TWICE CONDEMNED

IRISH VIEWS OF THE DREYFUS AFFAIR

RICHARD BARRETT

ORIGINAL WRITING

978-1-907179-95-2

A CIP catalogue for this book is available from the National Library.

Published by ORIGINAL WRITING LTD., Dublin, 2010.

Printed by CAHILL PRINTERS LIMITED, Dublin.

Acknowledgements

My thanks go to Dr Stephen Lalor and Deirdre Behan for their invaluable help and advice, to Dr Patrick Maume and Frank Callanan for dealing with my queries, to Fionnuala Ni Casadaigh for translating from the Irish, to Garrett Bonner and Steven Weekes for all their help with publishing, and, last but not least, the staff of the National Library of Ireland.

CONTENTS

Alfred Dreyfus: the French Captain whose conviction for treason sparked the greatest political scandal of the late 19th century

ABOUT THIS BOOK

This is a very short and simple book. It is a survey of opinions expressed in the columns of Irish newspapers and magazines on the Dreyfus affair while that unique controversy was at its height in the late 1890s. I believe that there are good reasons for looking at this. Discussion of how the Dreyfus affair (or the "*affaire*") was seen in Ireland can give us valuable insights into a number of topics, including Irish views of French and World affairs as well as the make up of nationalism, unionism, sectarianism and anti-Semitism inside Ireland itself.

The book's contents are based mainly on a study of a number of Irish newspapers and magazines of the time, from all parts of the island and of the political spectrum. This includes all the major national newspapers and a selection of provincial ones, plus religious and political periodicals. It is possible that one or two revealing pieces of writing have been missed, particularly if these were in one of the provincial papers not selected for this study. However, the study still does present a representative and high-resolution picture of the state of Irish public opinion.

The book focuses on discussion of the *affaire*, rather than reportage of it. Almost all national dailies and some provincial papers contained extensive factual reports of the *affaire's* progress, usually supplied by commercial wire services such as Reuter's. Such syndicated reportage informed the debate in Ireland, but does not tell us what people in Ireland were thinking or writing or why, which is the focus of this piece of work.

The principal time focus is on the period of the affaire's greatest controversy and divisiveness, namely from early Spring 1898, when Émile Zola wrote his explosive piece *J'accuse*, to Autumn 1899 when the Second court-martial of Dreyfus took place at Rennes in Western France.

There was originally an intention for this work to encompass material from non-periodical sources such as memoirs, biographies and records kept by organisations. However, an examination of some materials of this type showed that references to the *affaire* were too few and far between to justify the considerable additional time it would take to find and incorporate them. Nevertheless, a few such sources have been used.

Finally, it should be noted that part of the subject of this book has already been covered in my article "The Dreyfus affair in the Irish nationalist press, 1898-99" in *Études Irlandaises* 31/1, Spring 2007.

Richard Barrett

August 2010

Émile Zola:
The novelist whose explosive article 'J'accuse' blew open the scandal

THE *AFFAIRE*

This section of the book is intended as a general introduction to the Dreyfus affair and to the milieu in which the affair was debated, in France and elsewhere. Readers who are already knowledgeable about the *affaire* and reactions to it may feel they can move on to the next chapter.

The *affaire* itself originated in the arrest in the Autumn of 1894 of Alfred Dreyfus, a Captain in the French artillery serving at the time at military headquarters in Paris. Dreyfus, who was from a wealthy Alsatian Jewish family, was charged with passing sensitive military information to the German embassy.

It is true that good information was being sent by someone to the German embassy. Cleaners in the embassy did routinely pass items from embassy waste paper bins over to the French army's "Statistical" (in reality, intelligence) section, and the "smoking gun" in this instance was a memorandum (or *bordereau*), the writer of which offered to supply the Germans with documentation on a number of French military secrets and which was signed with the letter "D."

Senior officers were quick to suspect that Dreyfus, who was then working in an area from which the sort information given in the *bordereau* could be taken, was the traitor. This was partly on the basis of his Jewishness, which was certainly held by many, in the army and elsewhere, as an indication that he was not truly French. The fact that he was also from a province (Alsace) that had come under German control after France's defeat by Germany in 1870-71 cannot have helped.

Dreyfus was a junior officer who had embarked on an elite career path, but whose Jewishness had already caused him a problem when he had had to complain of low marks given to him and another Jewish officer at the Ecole supérieure de guerre. In October 1894 he was asked to come into work in civilian attire and was asked to take dictation from an officer who read out part of the *bordereau*. Dreyfus was then told that his handwriting did indeed match that on the *bordereau*, was arrested for treason, interrogated and held in military prison. Almost immediately, this fact was leaked to elements in the anti-Semitic Paris press.

Dreyfus was court martialled for treason in a highly secretive trial in which his defence counsel was not allowed, for reasons of "national security," to see, or even to know about, a dossier of evidence used against him. Handwriting evidence was also used, but the experts consulted were not unanimous. Inconsistencies in handwriting analysis were explained by the convoluted theory that Dreyfus had tried to distort his own writing to give the impression that someone was imitating him in order to frame him. As there was no longer a death penalty for his crime, he was sentenced to life imprisonment and, after a ceremonial degradation and expulsion from the army in January 1895 (during which he loudly protested his innocence), he was sent to Devil's

Island off the coast of French Guiana. There he was held in his own compound under constant surveillance, and was not allowed to keep abreast of developments at home.

These events took place in a period when France was still smarting from defeat by Germany in the war of 1870-71, and when anti-Semitic conspiracy theorists, such as Edouard Drumont and his paper *La Libre Parole* were enjoying great popularity. Two financial scandals, the collapse of the Catholic-run *Union générale* bank in 1882 and the scandal which enveloped the Panama Canal Company in 1889, had been widely attributed to Jewish machinations. Indeed up to this time, many on both the political left and the right accepted the popular stereotype of the Jews, of whom there were about 80,000 in France, as parasitic, wealthy cosmopolitans who lacked loyalty to their native country.

France in the 1890s seemed to be finally settling into a stable republican regime. The fate of the Third Republic, founded amid the chaos of defeat to Prussia in the war of 1870-71 and the bloodbath of the Paris Commune, had often appeared to be in the balance. Attempted royalist revivals in the 1870s had come close to success, and the abortive movement to bring about a coup d'état to be led by the popular General Boulanger in 1889 were still recent memories. However, if the republic now seemed destined to stay, it had within its body politic a range of forces, Royalist, Bonapartist, Boulangist, conservative Catholic, all often anti-democratic and usually anti-Semitic, who would not rest content with a liberal or secular political culture, and who were open to finding ways of challenging, if not subverting, French liberal republicanism.

Following on the verdict against Dreyfus his family, particularly his wife Lucie and his brother Mathieu, engaged themselves in heroic attempts to find evidence that would exculpate Alfred, but this quest was itself used by some anti-Semites to feed allegations about a huge conspiracy by powerful Jewish interests who were prepared to subvert Army justice. In any event, the case against Dreyfus began to unravel when another message, in the same handwriting as the *bordereau*, was found in the German embassy waste paper bins in 1896, while Dreyfus was imprisoned on Devil's Island. An officer, Georges Picquart, managed to unearth evidence that another officer, the (non-Jewish) Major Walsin Esterhazy was the real traitor. However, his superiors, instead of encouraging this line of enquiry, hastily despatched Picquart on assignment away from Paris. After Esterhazy demanded the right to clear his name, he was acquitted of involvement by a biased Court-Martial in early 1898.

It was from this point that the *affaire* began to develop into a national convulsion. The novelist Émile Zola, already no stranger to literary and artistic controversy, published his classic article *"J'accuse"* in the liberal journal *L'Aurore*. In this article he "named and shamed" a number of figures in the French army and political establishment, accusing them of colluding in a miscarriage of justice. Zola was then successfully prosecuted for criminal libel and fled to England, but not before a substantial proportion of the liberal intelligentsia had rallied to the previously marginal Dreyfusard cause.

At the other extreme, the mob in Paris and other cities at times seemed to be baying for the blood of Dreyfus, the Jews and now the intellectuals as well. Powerful groups within the Catholic Church, especially the Assumptionist order and its paper *La Croix* spoke out against the perfidious influence of Jewry. Within the Church, anti-Semitism tapped into hostility to liberalism and to the Republic, notwithstanding the *Ralliement*, the new climate of accommodation to the Republic which now held sway in most of the French Church. For many in France, the attempt to vindicate the innocence of Dreyfus was a threat to the honour of the Army and the cohesiveness of the nation, and for right-wing intellectuals like Charles Maurras, the founder of *Action Française*, the objective truth or justice of the *affaire* was of lesser importance than the integrity of *la patrie*.

The discovery in Summer 1898 that a key document from a secret dossier which had supposedly copperfastened Dreyfus's guilt was in fact a forgery (and the subsequent suicide of its author Major Henry, a devoted supporter of the General Staff) helped bring Dreyfus's case to the country's principal court of appeal, the *Cour de cassation*, who ordered a repeat court martial of Dreyfus. The convict was brought back from Devil's Island and the new trial took place, under the full glare of the world's press, at the Breton city of Rennes in August-September 1899. The verdict was again guilty by a majority of 3 votes to 2, but the military judges found "extenuating circumstances" (rather unusual in treason cases) and reduced Dreyfus's sentence. The judgment was swiftly telegraphed worldwide, reaching most of the world at almost the speed of the O.J. Simpson verdict of a century later, and in most cases, outside of France itself, to reactions of disgust and scepticism.[1] In the English speaking world and in Protestant countries, outrage at this evident travesty of justice was unanimous, being only a little more muted in Catholic publications. In a number of countries, French citizens became targets of abuse, and in Britain and America, there were moves to boycott the planned Paris exposition due in 1900.

In the event, the by now widespread disbelief in Dreyfus's guilt, and the changing political complexion of French government, led to Dreyfus's pardon in late 1899, a pardon which Dreyfus only reluctantly accepted as it did not clear his name. Those implicated in the *affaire* were amnestied. The complete exoneration and restoration of Dreyfus to the Army came in 1906. Dreyfus retired from the army in 1907 but returned to serve with the colours in the First World War. He died in 1935.

The world's attention turned from the *affaire* very soon after the Rennes verdict. The international boycott of the Paris exhibition did not materialise, as the rapidly developing South African conflict turned the world's attention elsewhere. [2]

What, then, was the nature of the ideological civil war which the *affaire* represented? It is usually seen as a battle between two visions of France – one liberal, universalist and anti-clerical, the other traditionalist, non-republican and frequently anti-Semitic. By the time the *affaire* reached its height in 1899, public opinion in France and in much of Europe tended to divide fairly neatly between conservative "Anti-Dreyfusards" and liberal "Dreyfusards" with Catholics usually being identified with the former position, while liberals and socialists were almost all of the latter.

However, in close up, the picture was more complicated than that. British support for Dreyfus, for example, probably stemmed from more than just the Anglo-Saxon sense of fairness in which British writers took great pride. Britain and France were in a period of exceptionally poor diplomatic relations in the 1898-99 period, culminating in the confrontation in Fashoda in Central Africa, where French territorial ambitions had been frustrated by a show of British power. Sections of British public opinion were also receptive to prejudiced approaches to French affairs, particularly if this included a chance to attack French, or indeed any, Catholicism.

Also, and possibly surprising to modern readers, might be that fact that socialists and others on the left were slow to come round to Dreyfusism, choosing at first to regard the *affaire* as a squabble among the Bourgeoisie and of no interest to the working class, and many also shared popular prejudices towards Jews. However, by the end of the *affaire*, most socialists had awakened to the threat of anti-Semitism and for the need, on occasion, to make allies of liberals. Catholics, too, were not uniform in outlook; and several Catholic intellectuals took the Dreyfusard side.

7

British interest in the Dreyfus case, as in most countries, only became significant from early 1898, the period of *J'accuse.* There was undoubtedly a mood in Britain at that point that was critical of French militarism after the Anglo-French confrontation at Fashoda, and which was therefore prepared to believe the worst about injustice and incompetence in the higher reaches of the French army. Combined with this was a perhaps complacent belief that British standards of justice and fair play would make a Dreyfus case impossible in England, an attitude which Irish nationalists like Davitt felt themselves in a strong position to criticise.

As one writer has noted[3], the Dreyfusards were seen in England as something of an Anglo-Saxon cause, while the anti-Dreyfusard cause could be associated with "that lack of manly spirit which made possible the infamies of Jacobinism and the brutalities of Napoleonic tyranny." [4] Anti-Catholicism was bound to be at least a peripheral part of such a mix: "... it was handy to have a present-day reminder of the horrors of popes, Jesuitism and the inquisition."[5] Nevertheless English Catholicism, as represented by Cardinal Vaughan and the *Tablet,* was also mildly Dreyfusard. It seems that within Britain, almost the only critics of the Dreyfusard consensus were the Marxist Social Democratic Federation, and, by repute, some sections of the Irish Catholic community.

The pattern of opinion in England was largely repeated in the United States, where outrage at the treatment of Dreyfus was universal. The Catholic press did not challenge this consensus, but chose instead to play up the horrors of anti-Catholic activity in France and the dangers posed to Catholic property by extremist use of the *affaire*.[6] In Australia, there was also a significant divergence between the approach taken by Catholics to the *affaire* as against that taken by others, and again the Catholic press, which had a predictably strong Irish influence, played down the injustice done to Dreyfus and played up a "what about the Irish" angle, which emphasised the hypocrisy of the British, who had treated Irish political prisoners unjustly.[7] In Canada, the English-speaking press replicated the pattern in Britain and the US, while the Francophone press, influenced by a form of Catholic nationalism similar to Ireland's, showed anti-Dreyfusard and anti-Semitic tendencies.[8]

Most of European opinion divided along Liberal-Conservative lines, but Dreyfusard sympathies tended to win out as the affaire dragged on. By the time of the Rennes verdict, it would be safe to say that in almost all areas, typically only anti-Semites and certain sections of conservative Catholic opinion adhered to the anti-Dreyfusard cause.[9]

The pattern in Ireland, as we shall see, was not typical.

Endnotes

1 See for instance Denis, M., Lagree, M., Veillard, J-Y (eds) *L'affaire Drey-fus et l'opinion publique en France et a l'étranger* (Rennes: Presses Univer-sitaires de Rennes, 1995)

2 The above account is very basic. Those wanting a fuller account could usefully get hold of Ruth Harris's recently published account *The man on Devil's island: Alfred Dreyfus and the affair that divided France* (London: Allen Lane, 2010)

3 Tombs, Robert "Lesser breeds without the law": the British establish-ment and the Dreyfus affair 1894-1899 in *Historical Journal* 41 (2) 1998, p.495-510

4 *"Times"* quoted in Tombs, op cit. p.505

5 Tombs, op cit. p.506.

6 See Feldman, Egal, *The Dreyfus affair and the American conscience, 1895-1906*, (Detroit: Wayne State U.P., 1981) particularly p.123-145

7 See Thornton-Smith, C. Reactions of the Australian Catholic press to the Dreyfus case. *Australian Jewish Historical Society Journal,* 1997 (14), 57 at 64

8 See Senese, P.M Antisemitic Dreysusards: the confused Western Canadian press and Brown M. From stereotype to scapegoat: Anti-Jewish sentiment in French Canada from Confederation to World War 1, Both in Davies, A. (ed.) *Antisemitism in Canada: history and interpretation* (Waterloo, Ont: Wilfrid Laurier University Press, 1992). Canadian-Irish parallels are discussed in more detail in the concluding chapter.

9 See Brennan, J. F. *The reflection of the Dreyfus affair in the European press, 1897-1899* (New York: Peter Lang, 1998).

Irish anti-Dreyfusards (1)
Maud Gonne financed Arthur Griffith's anti-Semitic
United Irishman.
(With permission of National Library of Ireland)

IRELAND AT THE TIME OF
THE *AFFAIRE*

I reland during the period of the *affaire* had a divided but rapidly changing social and political landscape.

Irish politics in the late 1890s, particularly on the nationalist side, were undergoing a process of fragmentation and re-alignment. This period has often been characterised as one of widespread disillusionment with constitutional politics and of a corresponding interest, in some quarters at least, in more radically nationalistic politics, with a greater emphasis on language, race and culture and less faith in direct political action to right Ireland's wrongs.

Throught this period, the Irish home rule party dominated the country's electoral landscape, holding over ¾ of Ireland's 101 seats in the Westminster House of Commons. This party was a coalition of land reform agitators, republican Fenians and constitutional reformers with a strong rank and file base among Catholic small businessmen and farmers. Priests were generally expected to chair local meetings. Its constitutional programme was centred on home rule, an arrangement roughly comparable to present day Scots devolution or Catalan regional government. Its leader up to 1890 and "uncrowned king of Ireland" was Charles Stewart Parnell.

The involvement of Parnell in the divorce case between Captain O'Shea and his wife Catherine "Kitty", Parnell's mis-

tress, occasioned a bitter and poisonous split in Irish nationalist politics. On one side of the split was the defiant Parnell and
his loyalists, together with some Fenian and radical nationalist
elements who were to play a decisive part in the radicalisation
of Irish nationalism in the years ahead; on the other side were
the Catholic clergy, the pragmatic nationalist establishment
and their allies the British Liberals, themselves dominated by
religious nonconformists who could not tolerate Parnell's behaviour.

Parnell died in October 1891, but by the aftermath of the
1892 General election, the party had solidified into 2 major
factions: the majority Anti-Parnellites and the much smaller
Parnellite party, which had only 9 M.P.s. In addition, the larger party was itself divided into factions led by John Dillon and
Timothy Healy. Of these, the Healyite faction was considered
to be closest to the Catholic clergy. By the later 1890s, two
home rule bills had failed to get passed by Parliament and,
with a Conservative administration in power, there was no
immediate prospect of progress in that direction. "The party"
was coming to be seen less as a radical popular movement
and more as an entrenched political machine, most of whose
members were, from 1898, organised through the United Irish
League.

The choice of "United Irish League" as the name for a new
nationalist organisation was significant. The year of *J'accuse*,
1898, was also the centenary of the bloody insurrection of
1798 which had been led in most areas by the United Irishmen, devotees of French-style republicanism. There were a
number of nationalists intent on using the centenary to popu-

larise a nationalism that was more resolutely separatist and more centred on cultural and racial identity than on political or economic grievances. Reflecting this, a Gaelic linguistic revival was well under way, as was the so-called "Celtic twilight" movement in Ireland's English language literature, exemplified by the romantic and semi-mystical imagery of W.B. Yeats.

Already prominent among the advanced nationalists was Dublin Parnellite Arthur Griffith. Griffith was a radical separatist, though not a republican, who wished Ireland to emulate Hungary's success in becoming part of a dual monarchy as it had done in the form of the Austro-Hungarian empire. This kind of separatist thinking had a following in the young Catholic middle class, many of whose most intelligent members were attending University College Dublin. A much weaker movement in the Irish context was socialism, whose main proponent was Glasgow-born James Connolly and his tiny Irish Socialist Republican Party.

Republican activists, whether involved in constitutional politics or not, were often members of the Irish Republican Brotherhood. These activists had keen memories of the harsh and unjust treatment of their members at the hands of British police and judiciary, which was bound to give them a jaundiced attitude to British interventions on the side of justice in other countries.

Unionism, that is, loyalty to the United Kingdom and opposition to home rule or independence, was the other major feature of the Irish political landscape. In Ulster it was politically dominant, had a following in all classes, was enmeshed with the Orange Order and was utterly intransigent in the face of home rule. Outside Ulster, a less strident form of unionism was still the preference of Protestants, who were mainly middle class and were strongest in cities and large towns. Catholic and Protestant communities both contained elements which emphasised difference and apartness, whether in the form of Orange anti-Catholicism or of Catholic insistence on denominational education. These factors would also influence varying responses in Ireland to the *affaire*.

Ireland suffered from recurring communal problems of sectarianism in the North and of sectarian/class tension in the rural South, and so popular anger, when directed against "the other" had for some time had ready outlets other than Jews. Before about 1880 the Jewish presence had not been significant, but there was a growth in Jewish numbers in Dublin and some other towns in the later 19th century, following on pogroms within the Russian empire.

The circulation of a letter of 1890 addressed "To our English co-religionists" from members of the Dublin Jewish community indicated that Dublin Jewry consisted of about 12 families of English speaking Jews of long standing, plus between 600 and 700 more recent arrivals, who had fled after 1881 from pogroms in the East, especially Lithuania.[1] By 1901 there were a little under 4000 Jews in Ireland, the biggest concentration being in Dublin, with a couple of hundred each in Belfast, Limerick and Cork.[2] In the cities, Jews were often shopkeepers and garment workers; elsewhere, many were itinerant pedlars.

Very few Jews in Ireland were at this stage rich or politically influential, though Belfast elected a Jewish, and Unionist, mayor in 1899. Interestingly, Dublin Jewish voters too were generally believed to be unionist supporters.[3]

Incidents of anti-Semitism were sporadic and most were quickly denounced by politicians (including Michael Davitt) and press (including the *Freeman's Journal*.)[4] The only serious anti-Semitic incident in Irish history is the Limerick boycott of 1904, when much of that city's Jewish community left the city on foot of a boycott instigated by an anti-Semitic Redemptorist priest.[5] This boycott received no support outside Limerick. Otherwise, Irish attitudes, such as they were, to Jewish matters, were tolerant and indifferent. The absence of mass anti-Semitism could arguably be quite well accounted for in the cynical words of Mr Deasy in the "Nestor" episode of Joyce's Ulysses, who explains the lack of persecution of Jews in Ireland to the fact that Ireland never let Jews come in the first place. [6]

France was a complicated entity in the Irish nationalist mind. For most of those with a Catholic education, Catholic France had been the hope and ally of Catholic Ireland for centuries past. One problem here, however, was that it was the revolutionary and republican France of the 1790s, under a regime actively opposed by the Catholic Church of the time, which had inspired and succoured the United Irishmen whose anniversary was being widely marked in 1898. It might be said that advanced Irish nationalism was uniquely and simultaneously trying to embrace the revolutionary liberal nationalism of Mazzini while also instinctively sharing the popular reverence and affection for the "Saggart aroon", the priest suffering with his faithful flock. In these respects it was a movement considerably removed from the bourgeois liberalism of England, and also from the divisions between Catholic conservatism and anti-clerical liberalism which was common in most Catholic countries.

At the time of the Franco-Prussian war of 1870-71, it was remarked that Irish opinion was more sympathetic to defeated France than was the case in England.[7] This was almost certainly, at least in part, out of a sense of solidarity with Catholic powers. We can also see this tendency to identify with Europe's historic Catholic nations in the support given at this time by John Redmond to France at the time of Fashoda,[8] and by Irish nationalist papers to Spain in her struggle with the United States in 1899, a position which was shared by the Irish-American press.[9]

Ireland's newspapers were undoubtedly of mixed quality, but Irish readers certainly lacked for nothing in quantity and choice. In 1885 for instance, the Provincial Newspaper Society had 265 member papers in Ireland.[10] Most of these were family owned, some having circulations of less than a thousand, others having five-figure readership estimates.[11] Most newspapers published in Ireland in the period 1885-1910 were in fact established in that same period.[12] Irish literacy rates were estimated at 75%, and Dublin Castle reckoned that nationalist papers were heavily read by the politically influential farmer, shopkeeper and labourer classes.[13] It has also been remarked that in Ireland of the time "Buying a nationalist newspaper was, in its own right, a political act, and in that sense Irish newspapers were not simply the medium through which politics were reported: to a certain extent, Irish newspapers *were* politics."[14]

Ireland, therefore, had a literate and politically interested population, probably more than was the case in many other European countries, especially Catholic countries, at that time, and which was served by a vibrant and diverse press. At the same time it had a resurgent Catholic Church that was in tune with popular political currents such as nationalism, rather than being in opposition to these as was the case in, for example, Italy. Inter-communal tensions in Ireland had sectarian rather than ethnic or class outlets, and a history of widespread anti-Semitic activity was absent. An Irishman's views of world affairs were far more likely, if a choice was necessary, to be decided by his attitude to England than by his attitude to Jews.

It now remains to see how the Dreyfus *affaire*, and its significance, was discussed within this untypical society.

Endnotes

1 See Shillman, Bernard, *A short history of the Jews in Ireland*. (Dublin: Cahill/Eason, 1945) p.98

2 See Keogh, Dermot and McCarthy, Andrew *Limerick boycott 1904: anti-Semitism in Ireland* (Cork: Mercier Press, 2005) p.3-4.

3 See *Freeman's Journal* 22 January 1898, where Jewish voters in one city ward are counted as probable unionists. O'Grada attributes this tendency to a rabbinical principle of loyalty to the governments of adopted homelands, coupled with a fear of nationalist Xenophobia. See O'Grada, C. *Jewish Ireland in the age of Joyce* (Princeton University Press, 2006) p.188-189.

4 See Keogh and McCarthy, *op cit*. pp.14-17

5 See Keogh and McCarthy, *op. cit.*

6 Joyce, James *Ulysses* (Bodley Head 1960 text, Penguin 1992) p.44.

7 For example see J. De L. Smyths's introduction to Duquet, A. *Ireland and France* (Maunsel, 1916) p.xiii.

8 See *Irish Daily Independent*, 22 October 1898.

9 For example see *Irish World* (New York) 12 August 1899.

10 See Legg, Marie-Louise *Newspapers and nationalism: the Irish provincial press, 1852-1892* (Dublin: Four Courts, 1999) p.126.

11 Legg *op cit* p. 127

12 Morash, Christopher *A history of the media in Ireland* (Cambridge U.P. 2010) p.116

13 Legg *op cit.* p.128

14 Morash, *op. cit.* p.117

Irish anti-Dreyfusards (2)
Arthur Griffith's views on the crisis in South Africa heavily influenced his anti-Semitism.
(With permission of National Library of Ireland)

THE VIEWS OF THE DUBLIN
NATIONALIST PRESS

The majority of Ireland's nationalist dailies were published in Dublin, which already functioned in many respects as a capital city (though obviously one without a
parliament), and Dublin's nationalist dailies can be safely
assumed to follow most closely the lines of the party factions with which they were associated. Dublin was also
the home of papers serving individual political or cultural
currents, including The *United Irishman* (separatist), The
Workers' Republic (socialist) and *An Claidheamh Soluis*,
(The Gaelic movement).

The *Freeman's Journal* was undoubtedly the main organ
of the Dillonite, or majority anti-Parnellite faction, while
the *Daily Nation* was the voice of the Healyites. Both had
weekly editions which differed only a little from the content or views of their daily stablemates. Dublin was also
the Parnellites' main stronghold, and was the home of the
Irish Daily Independent and the *Irish Weekly Independent*, which had been established by and for Parnellites. By
the later 1890s, the views of these two had begun to di-
verge, with the weekly paper arguably continuing with a
more specifically Parnellite tone.

In the early stages of the Dreyfus controversy, the principal Dublin papers carried syndicated reportage,[1] and
some discussion of political events in France[2], but the con-

demnation of a spy in the French army was clearly not considered a matter needing comment. However, later on, and in particular during 1898 and 1899, all these papers began to carry significant comment on the developing *affaire*. As we shall see below, the most common editorial line taken by Dublin's nationalist dailies was an opportunistic anti-Dreyfusardism in which France, or a certain understanding of France, was championed in order to score points against the hypocrisy which was seen as underlying British support for Dreyfus. In this sense we can see a quite discernible trend as the affair went on towards its climax at Rennes, evolving from a detached sympathy for the prisoner in 1898 and early 1899 towards a concentration on attacking British hypocrisy and, in tandem with this, defending the court martial and its verdict.

The *Freeman's Journal* gives a good illustration of this trend. Like most national dailies, the *Freeman* carried extensive accounts of the trials and associated events, mostly supplied by commercial wire services. A lot of comment was supplied by correspondents, e.g. "Paris notes" and "London correspondence."

The *Freeman's* pieces in 1898 initially had a moderately pro-Dreyfus tone. In January 1898 the *Freeman* called for openness from the French Government. "Dreyfus may be the greatest traitor an army or a nation ever knew. If so, let the case be proved. It is a mistake for the French Government to make their enquiries in the matter behind closed doors, because that breeds distrust." [3] Later the same month, the *Freeman* carried a sharp critique of French anti-Semitism, asserting that "... neither M. Drumont nor any other French anti-Semite has yet been able to prove conclusively to the impartial outsider that the average Jew of France was any bit more hostile to the interests of France than Lord Beaconsfield,[4] for instance, was to the interests of England." The editorial also expressed generous opinions of Zola who ...in the courageous action he has taken, speaks for a distinguished company ... [and] ...seems, so far as we can judge, to have the sympathy of thoughtful people in almost every civilised country in the world" [5]

On the other hand, another *Freeman* article a month later took quite a different view, holding that "What has irritated the French nation in connection with this whole matter is the belief that the agitation in favour of Dreyfus is the work of an enormously wealthy clique of Jews, acting in the conviction that their money, the ruling power in the world, can purchase anything, even the national conscience."[6] (The conflation here of "The French nation" with the anti-Dreyfusard part thereof was to be quite common in the Dublin nationalist press.)

By the time of the Rennes verdict, the *Freeman* was taking an even more markedly anti-Dreyfus line. An editorial just after the verdict entitled "Dreyfus condemned" endorsed the re-condemnation of Dreyfus and attacked the attitude of the British Press. "We may anticipate an outpouring of further vituperation upon France and the defenders of France as a consequence of the verdict." However, "Those who have no animus against France and no desire to see her defences undermined, her Generals humiliated, and her people defamed, will keep their temper and remember Burke's aphorism that it is impossible to indict a nation." Also,

> The English correspondents at Rennes were already deeply pledged to the doctrine of Dreyfus's innocence before the trial commenced. Their extracts from the evidence are tainted with this foregone conclusion, and in their comments they assume that all who are witnesses against Dreyfus are either knaves or fools, while all who are for him are entitled to the same credit as inspired Evangelists.[7]

The editorial stepped back from taking an anti-Semitic position and its comment on the Jewish aspect was to ask "Why the Jews as a nation should identify themselves with Dreyfus is not quite clear. Any nation may produce a black sheep, and if Dreyfus is guilty it no more discredits the Jewish people than Arnold's treachery disgraced America." The editorial concluded with a flourish: "An innocent man," says the "Figaro," when it hoped for a favourable verdict "is not condemned twice"; and Dreyfus has been twice condemned."[8]

The Parnellite/anti-Parnellite division in Nationalist politics was less clear cut in 1898-9 than it had been 6 or 7 years earlier, and new factions were forming within nationalism, but there were still important differences between the two sides of the Parnell split which were capable of influencing views on contemporary events. The leading organ on the Parnellite side was the *Irish Daily Independ-*

ent, but here too there was a fluctuation in sympathy away from an initially pro-Dreyfus position, albeit with a partial swing back again.

In January 1898, the *Independent* commented that "Whether Captain Dreyfus be guilty or innocent there is reason to fear that he was the victim of panic, and that, under the circumstances, his trial and conviction were unjust."[9] Most of the commentary in early 1898 issues was in a similar vein. For example in mid-February 1898 the paper said that the original Dreyfus court martial of 1894 was "a shocking travesty of justice" and went on to say that "unless legal tribunals in France are useless, M. Zola should be acquitted, and Dreyfus should be retried."[10]

However, *Independent* editorial comments later in February 1898, when Zola was charged with libel over *J'accuse*, adopted a much cooler tone towards Zola, whose expected stay in luxurious prison conditions was derided, and a notably anti-Semitic tone was introduced. The paper asked the question "...why is the Jewish race so much hated in France?" The article expressed the suppositions that there were 600,000 Jews in France whose usury was "devouring France" and that a syndicate of rich Jews was behind the pro-Dreyfus agitation. The article concluded:

> The populace do not care very much whether Dreyfus was guilty or not. Their antipathy to him is based on the fact that he is a Jew, and M. Zola, for having championed the cause of an ex-officer in the French Army who belonged to the hated race, has thereby earned unpopularity. It would

be wrong, of course, to assume that the populace is inevitably right in such matters, but on the whole, they are rarely wrong.[11]

In the later stages of the affair the *Independent*'s line softened a little. The paper for September 11 1899 carried an editorial entitled "The Dreyfus verdict." The editorial said that

To the majority of persons in this country who have followed the evidence as reported from day to day this verdict will undoubtedly seem unjust. It may be that the accused officer is really guilty or has been mixed up in a treasonable course of conduct, but the fact can scarcely be said to have been proved by evidence properly so called. [12]

However, the real nub of the editorial was on the behaviour of the English. "If we may judge from what has taken place, this verdict will excite wild indignation in England...For the last year and a half almost every organ of British opinion has been making the cause of Dreyfus its own." One or two London papers

... have indulged from day to day in a violent indictment of many of the chief men in France, and even of the French nation as a whole...By this course of action – which pleasantly assumed that England is free from reproach in the treatment of accused persons, and has, therefore, a right to lecture other nations on the subject – they possibly intended to help Dreyfus; but, if French feeling and opinion in the matter have been affected by their publications at all, it is absolutely certain that they have only contributed to and made certain his condemnation. [13]

In other words, English attitudes had provoked French bloody-mindedness and made things worse for Dreyfus. "If Dreyfus owes his fate to anything but the testimony given at Rennes he owes it to English advocacy."[14]

The *Independent* returned to the fray 2 days later in an editorial entitled "The campaign against France." "The English campaign against France continues to grow in virulence. Day after day the most violent abuse is poured by almost every journal in England not only on the heads of the French army, but on the French nation as a whole." The editorial described as "intolerable impudence" English plans to boycott the forthcoming Paris exhibition and to snub France in other ways. "So outrageous a piece of interference in the domestic affairs of a foreign country does not find a parallel even in the history of England." The "audacity" of England's behaviour "takes one's breath away."

Dreyfus may be the victim of injustice, but the last country in the world which ought to set itself up on a pedestal of virtue by indulging in such violent censures on any other as are now to be found daily directed against France is no other than England itself.[15]

An amusing footnote to the *Independent*'s coverage of the affair appeared on September 22. In the "Our mother tongue" column, the paper carried a piece which had appeared in the Gaelic League magazine, *An Claidheamh soluis*. It was a mock-dialogue in Irish on Dreyfus. The English translation, given alongside, gives this as a conversation between Tim and Denis. Denis asks Tim "Look here, Tim, do you think the people of France have any sense at all?" Tim says "What senselessness do you see upon them now?" Denis goes on to say that he has been reading of the trial of Drefus [sic], and that the trial consists of nothing but witnesses saying what they like about Drefus's guilt, and that being accepted.

> ...the public are worse even than the witnesses. ... they are ready to tear the windpipes out of each other with anger and rage, some of them saying that he is not [guilty], while there is not a single bit of proof at one side nor at the other upon the matter. They are an extraordinary description of people.

Tim says in reply that "No person rightly understands another's business. It is a person himself that knows when the shoe pinches."[16]

The *Irish Daily Independent's* evening stablemate was the *Evening Herald,* and this paper, whose comments on world affairs were shorter and pithier than those of the *Independent*, showed similar leanings on this issue. During the Zola trial in February 1898, the *Herald* gave the defendant no quarter. Pointing out that Zola's 1-year sentence was the maximum allowed, the Herald's "Current topics" column said that anything less than that

> ...would not have satisfied the Parisians, who looked on Zola's Libel on the army as an insult to the French nation, as it undoubtedly was. Zola's hatred of the French army is not the growth of yesterday. In his "Debacle" his attacks on it were of so malignant a character as to call forth a public protest from a gallant German officer who had fought against the French in the Franco-German war. Zola's recent performance was, on this account, rightly or wrongly, looked on by the French people as one inspired by a hatred of the army, and not by a desire to see justice done to a man whom he believed had been wronged.[17]

The *Herald's* attitude to the Rennes trial the following year was also entirely consistent with the line taken by the *Freeman* and *Independent,* and contained similar ingredients: cynicism about the English, plus an assumption that the French people were solidly against the prisoner, plus a plea for a limit to his suffering. The *Herald's* "Talk of the hour" column commented:

> For months the English Press were preparing us for a terrible outbreak in France whatever the result of the Dreyfus trial, but so far the verdict has been received calmly. From this it would seem as if outside the friends and partisans of the prisoner that the overwhelming majority of the French

people believe the decision is a just one and that his trial was fair. It is to be hoped, however, that the authorities may consider that he has been sufficiently punished and let the unfortunate man free. Unfortunately the insults hurled at France throw immense difficulties in their way of doing this.[18]

A cartoon in the same issue dealt with the idea of boycotting the 1900 Paris exhibition. It depicted Britannia saying "I'm thinking of boycotting the exhibition." Marianne, across the channel, cries "Boycott, boycott, boycott and all France will bless you" which was apparently an excerpt from a Frenchwoman's letter to the *Pall Mall Gazette*.[19]

The Healyite *Daily Nation* expressed a range of views similar to those of the other nationalist dailies. The paper's "Paris letter" column tended to be pro-Dreyfus. For instance in September 1899, commenting on declining local interest in the affair, Paris letter commented that "Outside of France ... few view so coldly a trial which, though transformed by Jews into a party question, is, after all, a mere matter of justice and humanity." Commenting on the well-known Jewishness of the editor of "*Le Gaulois*", a paper with an anti-Dreyfusard stance, the article remarked that "... a Jew who decries his fellow Jews is twice a Christian evidently." The same article also remarked that "Another curious feature of the affair is the way in which evidence that has been proved false or erroneous is still maintained by the Anti-Dreyfusards."[20]

However, most of the *Nation*'s editorial content on Dreyfus was very close to that in the *Freeman,* and at times a more definitely anti-Jewish note was struck. In 1898, he paper fulsomely backed the guilty verdict against Zola, and also forgave the wave of anti-Zola feeling at that time, saying that "...M. Zola has committed a grave and notorious offence against his country, and to demand that a warm-hearted people should make no avowal of their feelings would be to demand too much."[21] Also around that time, the *Nation*, debunking the forebodings of evil expressed in the British press, said that

> One is prepared to admit that France is capable of any-
> thing. The French Jews have been playing for big stakes
> recently. They have been checked, but not beaten. Every-
> thing will now depend on whether they pursue their ob-
> ject further. They are a stiff-necked race, and the wealth
> of France is in their hands. A stiff neck with an unlimited
> credit can accomplish much – even a revolution. ... Revo-
> lutions are bad for business, and Dreyfus must take a back
> seat when Hebrew business is endangered. It is certainly a
> serious evil that power so great to influence the destinies of
> France should rest in the hands of aliens, people devoid of
> patriotism or the national instinct.[22]

Later in 1898, at the time of Colonel Henry's suicide, the *Nation* backed calls for a retrial, but also darkly hinted that Henry's death might not be suicide at all: "There must have been many anxious to stifle a voice which had already uttered too much, and the tragic death of the General in the dungeons of the fortress of Mont Valérien may have been the penalty exacted for his lapse into honesty and candour."[23]

After the Rennes Verdict a year later, the *Nation* commented on the release of Dreyfus, saying that: "Most people will approve of the release of ex-captain Dreyfus by the French Government, no matter what their opinion as to his guilt may have been." However,

> The disgusting hypocrisy of the British attitude towards them [the French] since the Dreyfus verdict is not likely to be forgotten or forgiven by Frenchmen in this generation, and has wounded French public sentiment far deeper than even the Fashoda humiliation. It cannot be forgotten that the English Press is very largely under Jewish control... moreover it is a set part of British policy to discredit the French people, whose restless genius is regarded as a standing menace to British ambitions.

Also, "...it is necessary to remember that the telegraphic reports of the trial sent abroad from Rennes were utterly untrustworthy, all the testimony damaging to the prisoner being omitted or garbled." [24]

The editorial went on to give an alternative interpretation of the course of events. Contrasting Dreyfus's supposed conditions in captivity with the harsh regime suffered by O'Donovan Rossa, the article stated (very inaccurately) that

…Dreyfus … was allowed his coffee and cigars, his pomatums and fine linen, and given a much larger cell to live in than any Irish political prisoner in England, while he enjoyed a clime far superior to that of Portland or Dartmoor….So far… from believing that the prisoner's Jewish extraction led to his conviction, we hold that it had nothing to say to the case, while on the other hand we are satisfied that if the prisoner had not been a Jew, no fuss whatever would have been made about him, and he would have been left to rot in prison, or perhaps would have been shot as the result of his original condemnation.[25]

An important organ of nationalist opinion during most of the 1890s was *United Ireland*, whose views were usually in accord with the Dillonite wing of the Irish Party. *United Ireland* carried on a lively discussion of the *affaire* during 1898, but had ceased publication by 1899. *United Ireland's* own editorial line was critical of anti-Semitism, for example attacking militarism and persecution of the Jews [26] and accusing the French military of abrogating to itself the right to dictate to a court of justice.[27]

However, the same cannot be said for the contributor of the weekly (until March 1898) column "Some notes on public affairs" penned and signed by Frank Hugh O'Donnell, a former nationalist M.P.. O'Donnell expressed the same vituperatively anti-Semitic views which he would voice the following year in Griffith's *United Irishman*. O'Donnell had little time for Irish Dreyfusism, as we can see from his "notes" column of 21st January (around the time of the Esterhazy Court martial). In a section headed "The Anglo-Jewish treason and the Irish press" he said:"…the Irish daily papers, faithful to their mission of misrepresentation, carefully confined their notices to the reports of the Jew Reuter's telegraph agency and the comments of the English libellers of France, like the *Daily News, Daily Chronicle*, etc.", with the result that the Irish press "… represents nothing so much as a huge force-pump with the sucker in the English cess-pool and the nozzle in the mouth of the Irish public."

> The most satisfactory aspect of the Dreyfus treason is the manner in which it has led to the whole band of France's enemies, the Jews, the English, the Jacobins, the Communists, etc uniting to reveal their hatred of French religion and French nationality. … Besides the Freemasons and the Jews, we have Zola, the brothel novelist and blasphemous atheist, and the infamous Clemenceau, blasphemous atheist and Communist, whom the electors of the Gard hunted out of political life for his subservience to English designs against France.

O'Donnell continued by describing Esterhazy as a "most distinguished soldier" and hinted that it might have been England, not Germany, that was the real beneficiary of the treason.[28]

O'Donnell repeatedly made sure to put Zola, who as author of *J'accuse* had re-ignited the whole *affaire*, in his place. Zola, in O'Donnell's view, was not a Frenchman but the son of a Mazzinian refugee, and, moreover, the Zolas were *"Jews of Venice."*

> Zola, the rightful heir of a Venetian Ghetto Family, steeped in the traditions and sharing the blood of Mazzinians and Iscariots, is also the right man in the right place in pouring the sewerage of his repulsive mind upon Lourdes and Rome as well as upon the old Army of France in the centenary of Ninety-Eight.[29]

In early February, O'Donnell's comment on anti-Semitic rioting in Algeria, accompanied by moves to limit money-lending, was also quite unequivocal. In a "notes" item headed "France protects Algeria from the Jew usurers", O'Donnell declared

> The fierce outbreak of popular detestation against the Jew blood suckers of Algeria has caused the French government to intervene decisively against the usurious felonies of those vampires of mankind. The Jew must content himself with ten per cent at the outside, and proof of usurious habits will invoke fine and imprisonment.[30]

The removal of disabilities against Jews in France since the revolution was now, according to O'Donnell, a matter of widespread regret. Describing the way in which the Army officers had trapped Dreyfus in 1894, O'Donnell said

But Dreyfus did not stand alone. A whole tribe of Dreyfusites were his aids and screens, and France has now learned the invaluable lesson, which Russia, Germany and Austria [these countries did not allow Jews as officers] have long since learned, that the Christian Nation which trusts a race of *thieves and traitors* with the higher secrets of National Safety courts its own destruction.[31]

O'Donnell was not unchallenged on *United Ireland's* pages. Quite apart from the different tone of that paper's own editorial comment, O'Donnell found himself assailed twice by a correspondent signing himself (or perhaps herself) as "I.V.Y." who, in late February 1898, declared in a letter to the editor

Frankly, Sir, I am sick of Mr O'Donnell's ceaseless tirades against Jews and Freemasons – who seem to fill the same space in his imagination as "THOSE DREADFUL JESUITS" occupy in the minds of Ultra-Protestant old ladies… I am no lover of the Jews. A Jew candidate for Parliament or the Town Council would never receive my vote. But this is a frame of mind entirely different from the one that would deny to Jews their civic and political rights, that would inflame a race hatred against them, preach a crusade against them, hound them down, and generally make life as hard for them as possible. *That* frame of mind, unfortunately, appears to be Mr O'Donnell's as he pens his weekly *Juden-Hetze* for UNITED IRELAND.

I.V.Y. asserted Zola's Frenchness, saying that if Zola were not a Frenchman, then the Corsican Napoleon could hardly be seen as one either, noting as well that Esterhazy did not seem to be a particularly Gallic name.[32]

In a further letter not long afterwards, I.V.Y. took issue with O'Donnell's references to the Ghetto.

> The Jewish quarter ordained in Rome and other Italian cities was not an act of contumely, as he so absurdly implies. It was, on the contrary, an institution prompted by a Christian and humane motive – an intention that the Jews should not be scattered and consequently defenceless; but that they should have a quarter of the city entirely to themselves where, subject to certain regulations, they would be able to oppose a solid front to any mob that might desire (when inflamed by the O'Donnells of the period) to cut their throats, to loot their shops, and to violate their wives and daughters.[33]

To a charge made by O'Donnell that France was in thrall to 80,000 Jews, I.V.Y. said that if that was true of the French, then

> "…more fools they!" But I do not believe it, and I do not believe that the French are fools. On the contrary, I believe them to be a gallant and extremely shrewd race, amply able to take care of themselves as against the Jewish population of the entire world, even with the Freemasons thrown in. And I further believe that if the French countenance

military jurisprudence as exhibited in the Dreyfus-Zola cases and championed by Mr. F. H. O'Donnell, they will have a hole-and-corner oligarchy from which they will suffer more than from all the Jews and Freemasons that were ever born."[34]

I.V.Y's views are themselves very interesting to any student of anti-Semitism, for here was a liberal opponent of anti-Semitism asserting that he would never vote for a Jew, and that the ghettos of Europe were in fact an act of kindness towards Jews.

O'Donnell's "notes" column ceased in March 1898, and *United Ireland* itself was no longer published after the Autumn of that year.

The following year, however, Arthur Griffith, a Dublin printer and Parnellite, who was to become the founder of Sinn Fein, started to publish the *United Irishman*, a weekly paper financed by Maud Gonne, then living in Paris where she was the lover of Lucien Millevoye , a leading Boulangist and anti-Dreyfusard (and Iseult Gonne's father). *United Irishman* was dedicated to advanced separatism, and in its pages (in fact, usually on the front page) O'Donnell found a new home from which to spread the anti-Semitic word. Although this time his articles were headed "Foreign notes" and had the byline "The Foreign Secretary" instead of his own name, the similarity of style and content make these columns unmistakably his.

The "Foreign notes" column of 29 July 1899 is typical of O'Donnell's tone. In a section subheaded "The Dreyfus party plotting the disarmament of France," the writer asserted that Dreyfus himself was only a small part of the real issue. "For the Jews, of course, it is of supreme importance to secure the whitewashing of a Jew Officer who had been admitted so deeply into the military secrets of France, and they are spending millions to effect their object." Observing that Jews were not admitted to higher military rank in Austria and Russia, the writer considered that this

> …has nothing to do with their religious beliefs. It is rather
> a question of patriotism. The Jew has at heart no country
> but the promised land. He forms a nation apart wherever
> he goes. He may be a German citizen to-day, and a British
> subject to-morrow. … Touch a Jew in Warsaw, and collec-
> tions will be made to protect him in Moorish Synagogues
> on the edge of the Sahara and in Chinese Synagogues on
> the Yellow River. The French Army has sent a Jew to a
> convict settlement. So, woe to the French Army, if the Jews
> can manage it.[35]

The Foreign Secretary's most extreme invective was deployed on September 23rd, after the Rennes verdict. A London open-air meeting of support for Dreyfus was described thus:

> The Jews, who swarmed from their London ghetto into
> Hyde Park on Sunday, to rave out obscene insults against
> the French Army, were the loving comrades of a whole mob
> of blethering English agitators, Nonconformist tubthump-

ers, and Radical ranters, who howled against France and the French Generals with a low ferocity truly Anglo-Saxon. It was a sorry gathering. Some thirty thousand Jews and Jewesses, mostly of phenomenal ugliness and dirt, had come out of their East end dens at the summons of their Rabbis. If they hated France, it was also evident that they detested soap and water still more acutely. It was a scene to recall Thackeray's lines, how

"All the fleas in Jewry,

Jumped up and bit like fury."[36]

Not only Judaism, but Protestantism, or at any rate the wrong kind of Protestantism, attracted the Foreign Secretary's ire. On 25th November 1899, he brought together his grand theme of the triple evils of Judaism, Huguenotry and Freemasonry, evils which had their roots back in history.

The Jew's detestation of the Christian name is inflamed by the Jew's lust for gold and domination. The French Huguenot, unlike the patriot Protestants of Germany and Holland, still nourishes the gloomy fanaticism and the pro-English treachery which drew on Coligny and his sinister bands the subsidies of Elizabeth the Infamous and the loathing of the French Nation. The Freemason is but the instrument of Downing-street and the Synagogue, in whatever land he may "title" his burlesque, but dangerous, confederacies. The besotted Orangeman is the Huguenot of Ireland.

In other words, there was an acceptable kind of Protestant and an unacceptable kind, French and Ulster Protestants being among the latter. "Who has not seen the hand of the Jew, not to mention his nasal feature, in all the campaign of devilish mendacity which the Reptile Press of London and the Reptile Press of Dublin, nor of Dublin only, have waged against Justice and Liberty?" "The French Huguenot, like the Irish Orangeman, as if compact of some rank and noisome mould, is the slimy servant of his country's foe, and the bitter foe of his country's defenders."[37]

Another radical voice of *fin de siècle* Dublin was *Workers' Republic*, organ of James Connolly's Irish Socialist Republican Party. *Workers' Republic,* which began publishing in 1898 but which came out intermittently at times, did not comment extensively on the *affaire*. What comment it did have was heavily influenced by the opinions of European socialists, and especially by German Social Democrats, who were divided between those who saw the affair as an irrelevant squabble among the bourgeoisie and those who saw it as a worthwhile cause.

In October 1898, when the question of a retrial for Dreyfus was at the forefront, the *Workers' Republic* carried an instalment of its column "Men and opinions" which was signed by "The observer." This writer praised the Dreyfusard work of Zola and of socialist leader Jaurès, and attacked the role the Catholic Church in France was playing behind the scenes.

Speaking of the Dreyfus matter, many people in Ireland have been astonished at the way in which the clerical influence in France has been exerted against any retrial of the prisoner. The most violent and reckless of the anti-revisionist papers are those controlled by priests "whose black robes" says a writer in the *National Review* for October "are seen throught this vile business behind the bayonets of the War Office.

The writer then countered an accusation in *Reynolds News* that the prisoner's Jewishness was the key to the campaign for revision, but was "… in large part due, I should say, to that hefty and disinterested hatred of tyranny and injustice which we all have – when they are a long way off." Irish nationalists, including those whose main issue was with Britain, were no better:

The Irishman – if he is a capitalist – can boil over with patriotic rage at the Saxon swindling of the Egyptians or the Matabele – but he can go home with a light heart to lock out his own workers or pocket profits sweated out of the labour of women and children.[38]

On the 16th September 1899, *Workers' Republic* carried a critique of the *United Irishman's* anti-Dreyfusism. The piece was under the title "Home thrusts" signed "Spailpín,"(probably Connolly himself[39]) who said he had a "great respect" for *United Irishman*, which he found "fresh, breezy, readable and interesting." Spailpín did not attack Griffith's organ's anti-Semitism directly, but did accuse it of having done "all that men could do" to "estrange the sympathy of the French republican press from Ireland" by, among other things,

> ...senseless gibes about the "parliamentary republic" (whatever that may mean), by openly espousing the cause of the gang of Royalist conspirators who make the Dreyfus case the pretext for elevating the Army above the people, in order that the Army might be encouraged to destroy that safeguard of the liberties of the people, the Republic.

Spailpín went on:

> I allege this in full knowledge of the fact that, in consequence of numerous private representations as to the harm he was doing, the writer in question has, within the last week or two, been compelled to modify his language, and now hypocritically affects a solicitude for the welfare of the Republic.[40]

Other comment in *Workers' Republic* tended to be derived from views expressed by continental socialists. On 23rd September, there was a column headed "Fools or scoundrels? The Dreyfus court martial. What Jaurès thinks." This summed up the French socialist leader's views: "Clerical militarism has committed an unprecedented crime ... This is the first time that men, after a mistake has been recognised, have again sacrificed an innocent man. Henceforth, the caste which is capable of committing such a crime is outside the pale of humanity." The same page, under "Continental jottings" carried comments from the German Social Democratic paper *Vorwarts* inter-alia opposing the Paris Exhibition boycott. No views on Dreyfus's own guilt or innocence were expressed by *Workers' Republic* at this time, nor did it carry any attacks on alleged British hypocrisy.[41] Indeed at the end of 1899, the *Workers' Republic* carried a piece taken from the Brisbane *Worker* (from which other pieces had previously been taken) called "Suppose." This was a pro-Boer piece which would probably not score high marks for "political correctness" in more recent times:

> What would you do in the same position as the Boers? Supposing you were a proud and stubborn people, knit together by blood and kinship, and living under a kindly Government of your own, loyal and patriotic to it, and toward each other; suppose you had been moved on twice out of country you had conquered from savagedom; supposing it were not possible for you to move up any further, and that your country was invaded by a mob of Jew and foreign exploiters, who, gorging themselves upon its wealth, in their greedy desire to obtain the whole of it, succeeded in evoking the aid of the most powerful army on earth in enforcing their harassing and unrighteous demands – what would you do? Would you hand it over to them calmly like cowards, or stand by it like men? You would stand by it, you say. Well then, that is what the Boers are doing.[42]

In any event, there was still a minority Dreyfusard contingent in the Dublin nationalist press. This was well represented by the Parnellite *Irish Weekly Independent*, which departed from the more conservative views of its daily and evening stablemates on this issue. In the post-Rennes period, the *Weekly Independent* had an eloquent comment on the Rennes verdict in the form of a front-page cartoon. This showed Marianne, the mascot of the French Republic, dancing with 2 French officers, their backs turned away from a dejected, Dreyfus, his broken sword by his side. The caption read: "The honour of the army is preserved. Dreyfus has been found guilty and is to undergo ten years, imprisonment!" In the same issue, a forthright editorial intoned:

> The Nation that must bolster up an army or a constitution with human sacrifices [or] forgery is rotten; the "honour of the army" which needs dishonour and falsification to mend its tatters is in a sad plight. In all sincerity, but in sorrow and regret, we say we pity poor France to-day, our old time ally. France, once the home of chivalry and truth – to-day the mock of the civilised world.[43]

The *Weekly Independent* had in August given space to a lengthy letter from Arthur Lynch, who was later to be tried for treason for fighting on the Boer side in South Africa and later still became an M.P. Lynch, writing from Paris, wanted to warn Irish readers against being swept up in the pro-Dreyfus campaign being waged by the British media.

Lynch, no eschewer of the purple passage, spoke of England's true agenda as he saw it:

> The English hate France, and they want to teach the world to hate France. They hate the glorious history of France; they hate the free institutions of France; they hate the brilliancy and prestige of France; they hate the sacrifices that France has made for human liberty; they hate the Revolution of France; they hate the "Marseillaise"; they hate a people that exist without a House of Lords, and who do not know to bend the knee to royal shame; they hate the immortal page that France has written of American history; they hate Lafayette and Rochambeau; they hate the traditional friendship of France for Ireland; they hate Humbert, and Carnot, and Hoche; they hate Napoleon Bonaparte; they hate the name Republic.
>
> This is the reason they foster the Dreyfus agitation. This is the reason they make use of it as an instrument. This is why they seek to poison your minds. But they will not succeed. Irishmen, even when they do not know by virtue of facts and reasons, yet reach the truth by instinct. They pant and thirst for justice even as the hart panteth after water brooks, but they turn away from wells of English so defiled as that offered to them now by the British Press.[44]

Lynch's letter prompted an editorial reply in the same issue, which said that

No doubt England is all Mr. Lynch says, and more; but is that any reason that France should be excused for following so bad an example? Five hundred and five wrongs will not make one right, and France in this crisis must rise superior to any standard created by Great Britain.[45]

On the 23rd September the paper carried a liberal critique of European anti-Semitism entitled "Fear of the Jews." The article described the anti-Semitic climate in Russia, Austria and Germany, and noted that "In every country the Jews are accused of abrogating their duties to the countries they live in, and of acting together to further their own racial interests." However, "If calm consideration is given to all of this, one finds how difficult it is to maintain any of the charges so recklessly and so bitterly made against the Jewish race." Jews have "...never made the piles of your American oil kings and tinned meat emperors."

It is only an effete or degenerate nation that fears their influence or dreads offering them unfettered citizenship. They make good sons and husbands, good fathers and good mothers, and they are seldom found in police courts ... The Jews have been a persecuted race – so have we, and a little fellow-feeling, if not stern justice, should make us feel kindly towards a race that has borne and suffered as the Jews have done for so many centuries.[46]

The nascent Irish language revival movement was represented in print by *An Claidheamh Soluis*, published weekly from 1899 onwards by the Gaelic League. This paper had regular commentary on events abroad, particularly where there was a chance to comment on the behaviour of Britain.

On the 26th August 1899, events in France were discussed by An Conan Maol ("Bald Conan"), who expressed some sympathy for Dreyfus but also showed plenty of confidence in French justice. "It is fortunate for this man", said Conan,

> ... that there is a high court in France. We have no such thing here at home and if it were in this jurisdiction that he had been sentenced he would have remained convicted forever without rescue. There is good law in France and the man will get justice and fair play and rights. ... It is my prayer that this poor person will be freed if he is innocent, but it is difficult to say that he is and it is my opinion that he will be sentenced again and that he deserves it.[47]

Two further commentaries came from the pen of Ultach Beadaidhe ("The Ulster Gossip") whose identity is not known for certain, but who, in this author's opinion, was probably the then editor of *Claidheamh*, Eoin MacNeill.[48] In any case, this Ulster Gossip used a heavily ironic style with which to defend the French people, as he saw them, from vilification by the Jewish-controlled English press. Hence, on September 23rd, The "Gossip" wrote that

> The Jews are the wealthiest race of all, according to what

I hear. I wonder if it's true. It is the Jews who founded the major newspapers, [and] they who distribute world stories from country to country. If it is they who have paid the piper it is they who will give the tune a title and of course they do not like any song but the melody of truth. It is possible that a Jew would put a value of two pounds on a watch that is only worth two shillings. If you were wise enough you would get it for four shillings. But a Jew is the soul of truth if he is referring to another Jew.[49]

He then commented on how little the French people he met were actually interested in the case, though they seemed satisfied when the Rennes verdict came through. "Despite English, German and Italian journalists reporting, I am as certain as the French people are that Dreyfus deserved his sentence."

On The 30th, the "Gossip" wrote an endorsement of the Catholic view of France as a country whose good people were being ruled by an alien, irreligious element. The writer found the real French people he met on his travels to be more polite, more manly and more sober than those hinted at in the British press, but too willing to leave public affairs to the wrong element.

Most of the ordinary folk go busily and greedily about their work and leave the government to a group of rogues and to the Parisian mob. Most of the ordinary people have the Christian religion and they leave the government to a group without religion or more likely a group bitterly opposed to religion. As I hear, if anyone in the service of this government were seen going to Mass, or if his daughter were observed going to communion, it would be over for him. There would be no fair play or promotion to be had by him from then on.[50]

Overall, the Dreyfusard cause did not have an easy time of it in the Dublin-based nationalist press. This can be contrasted easily enough with the tone of the unionist press, but there are reasons why that would not be surprising. What may be more surprising is the contrast visible between views on the affaire expressed in the Dublin nationalist press and those which predominated in their provincial counterparts, as we shall see.

Endnotes

1 For instance the account of Dreyfus's ceremonial degradation in the *Irish Times*, 7th January 1895

2 For instance J.J. O'Kelly's discussion of French affairs in the *Irish Daily Independent*, 17th January 1995

3 *Freeman's Journal*, 21st January 1898

4 *Freeman's Journal*, 25th January 1898. Beaconsfield was Disraeli.

5 Ibid.

6 *Freeman's Journal*, 24th February 1898

7 *Freeman's Journal*, 10th September 1899

8 Ibid.

9 *Irish Daily Independent*, 22nd January 1898

10 *Irish Daily Independent*, 15th February 1898

11 *Irish Daily Independent* 26th February 1898

12 *Irish Daily Independent*, 11th September 1899

13 Ibid.

14 Ibid.

15 *Irish Daily Independent*, 13th September 1899

16 *Irish Daily Independent*, 22nd September 1899

17 *Evening Herald*, 2th4 February 1898

18 *Evening Herald*, 13th September 1899

19 Ibid.

20 *Daily Nation*, 4th September 1899

21 *Daily Nation*, 21th February 1898

22 *Daily Nation*, 1st March 1898

23 *Daily Nation*, 2nd September 1898

24 *Daily Nation*, 21st September 1899

25 Ibid.

26 *United Ireland*, 12th February 1898

27 *United Ireland*, 5th March 1898.

28 *United Ireland*, 22nd January 1898

29 *United Ireland*, 5th March 1898

30 *United Ireland*, 5th February 1898

31 *United Ireland,* 26th February 1898

32 *United Ireland*, 26th February 1898

33 *United Ireland*, 12th March 1898

34 Ibid.

35 *United Irishman*, 29th July 1899

36 *United Irishman*, 23th September 1899

37 *United Irishman*, 25th November 1899

38 *Workers' Republic*, 8th October 1899.

39 See Nevin, Donal *James Connolly: "a full life"* (Dublin: Gill and Macmillan, 2005) p.127

40 *Workers' Republic*, 16th September 1899

41 *Workers' Republic*, 23rd September 1899

42 *Workers' Republic*, 30th December 1899

43 *Irish Weekly Independent*, 13th September 1899

44 *Irish Weekly Independent*, 5th August 1899

45 Ibid.

46 *Irish Weekly Independent*, 23rd September 1899

47 *An Claidheamh Soluis*, 26th August 1899

48 MacNeill was an Ulsterman, and, like Ultach Beadaidhe was visiting France at that time. See also Tierney, Michael, *Eoin Macneill: scholar and man of action 1867-1945* (Oxford: Clarendon, 1980) p.68 and Martin, F.X. The writings of Eoin MacNeill in *Irish Historical Studies,* vol.6 no.21, March 1948 p.44-62.

49 *An Claidheamh Soluis*, Seacht-mi 23, 1899

50 *An Claidheamh Soluis*, Seacht-Mi 30, 1899. Trans by Fionnuala Ni Casadaigh.

"After the release of Dreyfus, France is still attacked":
Anti-Dreyfusard cartoon from Roscommon Herald,
23rd September 1899.
(With permission of Roscommon Herald.)

OUT OF TOWN DREYFUSARDS?
THE PROVINCIAL NATIONALIST
PRESS

One might expect the principal regional nationalist papers in the South of Ireland to echo the attitudes of Dublin papers such as the *Freeman*, but as we shall see not only was this often not the case, but there was, running through a significant part of this section of the press, sympathy for the Dreyfusard cause of a kind which owed little to secular liberalism as would have been understood by British or continental Dreyfusards.

A good example is the *Limerick Leader*, a nationalist weekly whose later coverage of the anti-Jewish boycott in 1904 did not cover it with glory, but which took quite an interesting attitude to this controversy. During 1899, the *Leader* touched on the affair in unusual ways such as in August, when there was a column called "Dryfuss," a burlesque spoof of the Rennes trial involving inebriated characters.[1] Later that month another piece of satire appeared, this time involving a Kafkaesque trial set in a French-occupied England in 1950. In this trial, prisoners were tried "in the French fashion", i.e. with hearsay permitted and without a presumption of innocence.[2]

On the 8th September the *Leader* had an editorial which said that the case against Dreyfus "would not be enough to hang a dog in these countries" and that "Dreyfus may be guilty, but to convict him again upon the evidence supplied by the heads of the army would be little less than assassination."[3] On the Rennes verdict, the *Leader* for 11th September had a short opinion piece which said "Whether Dreyfus is innocent or guilty cannot be determined as a result of the Rennes sittings, but that he has been convicted on wholly inadequate evidence is sufficient to justify the condemnation of the decision arrived at as a "criminal verdict.""[4]

Unusually for Irish papers, the *Leader* supported the Paris boycott call, describing the boycott idea as "... a policy which should recommend itself to every justice-loving man. France must be brought to her senses, and there could be no better way of showing her that she has merited the disapprobation of the whole world." [5]

Elsewhere in Munster, the *Cork Examiner*'s line was also Dreyfusard. The kind of thinking behind the *Examiner's* line was discernible in comments made on the 7th September favourably contrasting Irish life with that in South Africa and France, thus:

We have much to complain of politically and socially in this country. But be it always remembered we have much to be thankful for, thankful to the genius of our race, the honour of those who have gone before us, and to those to which belongs the guardianship of the religious instincts of the nation.[6]

In other words, the Irish race, and in particular Irish Catholicity, led by the Catholic clergy, contained a genius which stopped us from going the strife-ridden way of the French or South Africans. On 11th September 1899, in much the same spirit, the *Examiner* commented on the Rennes verdict:

> France the brave, the chivalrous, has paid a terrible penance for her determination to keep open old sores and to make her army the centre of all her hopes and aspirations. Her fate, in the eyes of the world, in the closing days of the nineteenth century is a warning to other nations of the penalties which may follow the gratification of the lust for conquest and the worship of the idols of Jingoism and Expansion.[7]

On the 20th September in a piece discussing the pardoning of Dreyfus, the *Examiner* carried a lengthy but articulate and interesting summary of this Catholic Dreyfusard position. In a sideswipe at much of the Irish press, the article commented "We are not aware that in any country, except France, and on one or two reckless occasions in our Irish Press, there has been a voice raised in support of the Rennes finding." The editorial then brought in aspects touching on Catholicism in the case. "His [Dreyfus's] conviction and sentence constitute a hideous and atrocious blunder, into which only a great nation like France could possibly have fallen. However, it was not the case itself but the subsequent commentary "which must have made

the blood of Catholics in every part of the world boil with
rage."

It has been the set purpose of English and Protestant journals ever since this judgment was pronounced to lay it
at the door of the Catholic Church, and to attribute the
outrageous proceedings of the courtmartial to the direct
instigation of the Jesuits. One would have fancied that we
had outlived these calumnies by some centuries. But they
are renewed in our time just as vigorously as in the good
old days of Titus Oates. The protest of the Pope, of Cardinal Vaughan, of every Catholic prelate of light and leading
that has spoken, goes for naught in the estimation of the
Protestant, who sets this Dreyfus scandal foremost among
the iniquities of Rome.[8]

The *Examiner* also carried two interesting views, which
were not its own, on the affair and issues arising from it.
One was Michael Davitt's attitude. The *Examiner* and
other papers carried much of the text of a letter Davitt
had written a letter to the *Westminster Gazette*. In this
letter, Davitt took the British press to task for its double
standards.

Supposing Dreyfus had been a poor man instead of
wealthy; the son of a French peasant instead of a rich Jew,
would your Press and pulpits and platforms pour forth this
torrent of tearful indignation over his fate? Not a bit of it.
… It is Dreyfus's racial position which has won him an

army of English sympathisers. Wealth always commends distress – flunkeries devotion. What angels of innocence you English are in your military and judicial records to fling your insulting imputations at a country which has risked and suffered more to elicit the real facts about the guilt or innocence of one man than England ever did or would risk for the fate of a thousand. Had Dreyfus been an Irishman, resident in Ireland in 1891, he might have been flung into prison without trial of any kind.[9]

The other piece, in the same issue as the Davitt letter, was a pseudonymous letter which contained that fusion of piety and economic opportunism for which conservative nationalism was to be pilloried by writers in later years. It was headed "Paris exhibition boycott. A chance for Irish manufacturers." The letter said that

> The Anglo-Saxon, Jewish, Masonic, and Nonconformist conspiracy against the French Nation, which has taken full advantage of l'Affaire Dreyfus, has apparently now resolved to boycott the Paris exhibition of 1900. Every Methodist, Wesleyan, Baptist and Presbyterian assemblage in Ulster, England, and the States abuses France, its army, its people, and its generals, together with the Society of Jesus, to the fullest extent of their capacity ... Are we, Irish Catholic Nationalists, going to stand by in silence and see a deliber-ate attack being made upon the Catholic Church of France, and the Catholic people of France, by persons whose own mansions want setting in order badly? I think it ought not

to be so, and I consider the best and most practical protest that can be made by Irishmen is to have our Irish manufacturers hasten during the present Anglo-Saxon boycott of the Paris Exhibition to offer their sympathy and services to the French people and try to secure the best places they can in the Exhibition.[10]

The *Kerry Sentinel*, a paper founded by the Parnellite Harringtons, was also stern in the cause of Justice to the accused, regardless of national politics. The *Sentinel's* post-Rennes editoral held that

> This verdict has disgusted the civilised world, and has made all true friends of France feel deep sorrow for the degeneracy which has overtaken her in a vital moment in her fortunes. … We can very well sympathise with the desire of the French people to see their army, which should be, and is, their glory and their pride, pure and uncontaminated. But the cause of justice is above and beyond all things, and in this case it has been sadly outraged.[11]

The *Waterford News*, also Parnellite, expressed similar sentiments, with a willingness to discuss Irish parallels, as it did on 22nd September 1899

> We have had traitors in Ireland, in times of trouble, but never at the worst stage of the informer cycle did we ever experience such an awful amount of treachery, unrelenting perjury, intrigue and absolute perversion of justice than

were manifest in the trial of the Prisoner of the Devil's Island.[12]

Significantly, the *News* chose to compare the treatment of Dreyfus and that of an Irish patriot not in order to attack British hypocrisy but instead to attack injustice in a more general way. Comparing Dreyfus to Thomas Francis Meagher, who had recently died, the editorial of September 22nd said: "We hold that there is an analogy between Meagher and Dreyfus. Both were men of undoubted probity and honour, and they were sacrificed by the lust for foreign gold, and the sanguine demand of a rotten system."[13]

Perhaps the most forthright exponent of Catholic Dreyfusardism was the fervently Catholic *Kilkenny Journal*. Its position was evident from the *Journal's* editorial of 26th August 1899 entitled "At the throne of Peter." This stated boldly that

Catholic Ireland is proud of its allegiance to the centre of Christendom, and Ossory [Kilkenny's diocese] is proud of being an ever faithful child of Him who rules in the Chair of Peter. ... What a pleasing change it is to turn from the sacrilegious devilry of France to the piety of this faithful land of ours! *La Belle France*, how it has fallen! How pitiable is its condition, bereft as it is of every redeeming character that should befit a nation! At present its concentrated energy is being devoted to the conviction of an innocent man. To save the Army or the incriminated heads of the General Staff anarchy has been let loose, and the gay city is now experiencing some of the worst terrors of the hateful commune.

At root, for this writer, was France's Godless system of education. France's convulsions were "an object lesson to those who hold that education and religious training should be separate. France is to-day paying the penalty of its blasphemous doctrines and infidel teachings."[14]

In 1898, the *Journal* had already flagged this point of view when an editorial penned after the Henry suicide suggested that

> The great Republic, with that freedom of opinion that at the time of the revolution recognized some men, but no God, is proving day after day that Monarchy may have its evils but that Republicanism can have more.... That the French government is rotten to the core is becoming more and more evident. That those high in state, especially those in military authority, are culpable to the last extent is plain, and that La Belle France has become a by-word amongst nations is incontrovertible.[15]

Soon after the Rennes verdict, the *Journal* commented that "The men who should be on Devil's Island are the majority of the Court that were cowed into sentencing him, and the pack of poltroon "generals" that gave evidence against him." On the boycott idea, the Journal said that "... we hope the movement will be a success, and that the

French people may be made feel that injustice, even to an individual, can be resented."[16]

The *Journal's* lack of sympathy with the "France right, England wrong" point of view of other nationalist papers was manifest in a comment a little later:

> England's interference has, of course, militated against the interests of Captain Dreyfus, but his sustainment by England is no justification for Ireland being a party to one of the most infamous judgements of the century. ... It is fulsome to read of this maudlin flattery of France. There has been a sentimental bond of sympathy between the two countries, but when it came to the spilling of blood, it was Irish blood that flowed in the service of France, and very little French blood that ever flowed in the service of Ireland.[17]

The *Journal* around this time also carried a pro-Dreyfus letter signed "An Ossory priest." The writer, who said he was ordinarily a *Nation* reader, congratulated the Journal on its "upright and manly stand in reference to the unhappy Dreyfus." Of the *Nation* and like minded organs, the writer said "To have acquiesced in the verdict, notwithstanding the opposite overwhelming conviction of the whole civilised world, to my mind seems stupid and absurd – I had almost said cowardly. Therefore, all honour to you, Mr Editor, for your noble defence of justice and truth."[18]

However, the Dreyfusards did not have it all their way in the provincial nationalist press, and (perhaps unsurprisingly) one can look Northwards to see a strong exception. The Ulster unionist press showed a tendency to combine the sense of moral superiority showed by the British press over the affair with a goodly dollop of anti-Catholic prejudice, and this found a robust antithesis in the line taken by the Belfast nationalist *Irish News*, particularly during 1898. The *News* was edited by Thomas Joseph Campbell, later a lawyer and Nationalist Stormont M.P.. In mid-February 1898, the *News* carried a fulsome defence of the verdict against Zola:

> Nothing has since [i.e. since the original conviction in 1894] occurred to induce the French authorities to believe there was a miscarriage of justice. The Jewish syndicates have raised the outcry that Dreyfus was wrongly condemned. Their newspapers repeat the cry with almost parrot-like docility. The honour of the army of the French Republic has been assailed. Of course the sanctimonious English newspapers ...are hypocritical in their denunciations of the ways of French Justice. And they have found an efficient ally in Zola, the author of scrofulous, anti-Catholic literature.

After remarking that "The Jewish side of the question is the only one that passes current in England" and accusing the Jews of being behind the Jameson raid in the Transvaal, the item went on to say that

The Jew is the ruler of all he surveys. He is hand in glove with the irreligious government which has engulfed the Republic in a mass of reeking scandals. They have absolute control of the country's finances. Since 1870 France has been absolutely at their mercy. What the Anti-Semites demand is special legislation that will make it impossible for the Jews to despoil the common people further, and will sever the tentacles which now have the revenues of France within their grasp. It is not an attack on the Jews as a race or as members of another religion. The Anti-Semites are strenuous in their advocacy of the equal protection of the law for Jews, but insist with vehemence that they be kept in their place, and subjected to certain necessary reforms, with a view to rendering them harmless.[19]

The discovery that parts of the dossier against Dreyfus were in fact forged, and the suicide of the forger Colonel Henry in August 1898, was reflected in a shift in the line taken by the *News*, which now supported a retrial for Dreyfus. After restating their belief in undue Jewish influence, the *News* accepted that there was a perception of "something unwholesome" in the atmosphere of the French army and politics, and said "If Dreyfus has been victimised, it will do honour rather than otherwise to his accusers to make amends by a revision of the trial."[20]

Opinions expressed in the *News* in the later stages of the affair in 1899 were a good deal blander, without any anti-Semitic content, and tended towards a lukewarm acceptance of Dreyfus's probable innocence, combined with the usual nationalist disdain for British and Unionist hypocrisy.[21]

There were a few nationalist provincial papers which did take the same line as the *Freeman's Journal* and the *Irish Daily Independent*, that is, concentrating on British hypocrisy and Pharasaism more than on the justice or otherwise of the treatment of Dreyfus. Carlow's *Nationalist and Leinster Times*, for instance, while not paying much attention to the affaire, did use it to attack British hypocrisy. A post-Rennes editorial jointly attacked British views of Dreyfus and of the Boers in a piece headed "The British Pharisee again."

> The latest opportunity which has been offered to him for self-glorification and the proclamation of his righteousness before men is the Dreyfus trial in France. He weeps tears over the unfortunate Jew Captain, expresses entire belief in his innocence, and indignantly denounces his corrupt and unjust judges. In fact to hear the worthy gentleman express his reprobation of judicial wrong-doing, one would never imagine he had any knowledge of a country called Ireland, or that such a thing as a miscarriage of justice ever took place beneath the folds of the Union Jack.[22]

At least one other regional nationalist paper did also come out unequivocally as both anti-Dreyfusard and anti-Semitic. This was the *Roscommon Herald*, run by Jasper Tully, anti-Parnellite M.P. for Leitrim South and a former political prisoner. The *Herald* chose, at the time of the

Rennes verdict, to defend the case against Dreyfus and to denounce the Jews. In an editorial comment published the week after the Rennes verdict, the *Herald* gave an uncritical summing up of the history of the *affaire* from an anti-Dreyfusard point of view, and presented this as the view "that has commended itself to nine-tenths of the French nation."[23] Bearing in mind that the French nation held Dreyfus as guilty of treason,

> ... it is necessary to examine the question of the religion of Dreyfus, which has been brought to play in the business. If Dreyfus were of the French race, and professing, say, the Catholic religion, both he and his crime would probably have been forgotten in a year or so after his conviction and deportation to a penal colony. Dreyfus is not of the French race, and he is a Jew. The manner in which the Jews stick to each other all over the world is strikingly exemplified in this case. The French call the Jews men without a country, and prepared to act for any country so long as they can make immediate pecuniary profits. The instinct of the Jew is to make money, and though he roll in wealth, when an opportunity occurs to make money, his instinct forces him to seize that opportunity at any risk. The Jews have united to a man in support of Dreyfus. It must be borne in mind that the Government in France under the Republican form has been largely in the hands of French Jews and French Huguenots. The scandals with which France has been threatened have sprung from Jews and Huguenots ... General Gallifet, the present Minister of War, is a man

of broken fortune, who is steeped to his lips in debt to the Jews. In fact the present Government is entirely committed to the Jew line, and as regards Dreyfus, it is only in direct opposition to them that he has been for a second time convicted. These facts show the power of the Jews at present in France.[24]

The same editorial went on to accuse the English of "arrant hypocrisy" given their treatment of Irish prisoners, and related how, apparently, Dreyfus was sent 500 Francs' worth of table delicacies every month by his wife while on Devil's Island.[25]

The *Herald* ran front-page cartoons in most issues, and the principal cartoon for its 23 September issue was headed "After the release of Dreyfus, France is still attacked." The picture showed a lion, marked "French Army" being set upon by dogs marked as "London Times" and "Standard" while Dreyfus was seen in the background being released by Marianne, the woman mascot of the French Republic. The caption read "Dreyfus having been pardoned, the Jew con-trolled [sic] Press of England is now going in full cry for the French Army."[26]

Further light on the *Herald's* stance is provided by another local paper, the *Roscommon Journal and Western reporter*, which reported on 30th September that Jasper Tully M.P., the *Herald's* owner, had been at the Rennes trial in person. The *Journal*, which carried no comment of its own on the Rennes trial, reported Tully as thinking that "there are strong grounds for believing that Dreyfus was guilty of treason and says that the anti-Catholic newspapers and news-agencies of Great Britain which are intensely hostile to France, never conveyed an impartial report of the proceedings or an accurate account of French feeling on the great "affair".[27]

We can see, without necessarily being able to explain, a significant difference between the balance of nationalist opinion in and outside Dublin. The Dublin nationalist press seemed to plump for an Anglophobic line of argument leading to an opportunistically anti-Dreyfusard stance, whereas the non-Dublin nationalist papers (including, in the later stages, even the more lukewarm example of the Belfast *Irish News*, in face of unionist taunting)[28] showed a preference for a pro-Dreyfus stance, but one inspired by a Catholic rather than a secular liberal perspective.

Endnotes

1 *Limerick Leader*, 14thAugust 1899

2 *Limerick Leader*, 21st August 1899

3 *Limerick Leader*, 8th September 1899

4 *Limerick Leader*, 11th September 1899

5 *Limerick Leader*, 13th September 1899

6 *Cork Examiner*, 7th September 1899

7 *Cork Examiner*, 11th September 1899

8 *Cork Examiner*, 20th September 1899

9 *Cork Examiner*, 16th September 1899

10 *Cork Examiner*, 16th September 1899

11 *Kerry Sentinel*, 13th September 1899

12 *Waterford News*, 22nd September 1899

13 *Waterford News*, 22nd September 1899

14 *Kilkenny Journal*, 26th August 1899

15 *Kilkenny Journal*, 24th September 1898

16 *Kilkenny Journal*, 16th September 1899

17 *Kilkenny Journal*, 20th September 1899

18 *Kilkenny Journal*, 20th September 1899

19 *Irish News*, 15th February 1898

20 *Irish News*, 3rd September 1898

21 For example *Irish News*, 13th September 1899

22 *Nationalist and Leinster Times* (Carlow), 16th September 1899

23 *Roscommon Herald*, 16th September 1899 (n.b. page incorrectly headed 23 September 1899)

24 Ibid.

25 Ibid.

26 *Roscommon Herald*, 23rd September 1899

27 *Roscommon Journal*, 30th September 1899

28 For example *Irish News*, 18th September 1899

THE VIEWS OF THE UNIONIST PRESS

Unionist newspapers existed throught the country, but Unionist daily papers with large readerships only existed in Ulster and Dublin. Most of the Irish unionist press took a pro-Dreyfus line, which accords with the behaviour of the English press, both Liberal and Tory, and bears out a correlation visible elsewhere in the world between Protestantism and support for Dreyfus.

Although the London *Times*, which was Dreyfusard and which ran a series on "The Roman Catholic Church and the Dreyfus case" in September 1899 was widely read in Dublin,[1] the Dublin *Irish Times* was undoubtedly the Irish unionist paper of record. During 1898, this paper more than once expressed serious concern about the extent of anti-Semitism in France. For instance, in February 1898, discussing the possibility of a pogrom, the paper commented that "The French seem almost prepared to carry a fanatical hatred of the Jew to an extreme so insane that none can tell what heinous and miserable consequence may not follow at any moment some accidental street manifestation of an uncontrolled and fiendish frenzy."[2] This editorial and others expressed doubt about the French Government's ability to control such passions. The *Irish Times'* reaction to the verdict against Zola placed little hope in the leadership of the French Government. In early1898, an editorial stated that "Those who attempt to criticise it [the verdict] are foredoomed to go to the wall under the present administration, and the existing blind fanaticism of public opinion." [3]

The following year, the *Irish Times* was equally forthright in its views on the Rennes verdict. An editorial a few days after the verdict observed the unanimity that existed in the English-speaking world's press: "We have printed in our columns extracts from many journals, not only published in the English metropolis, but in foreign capitals and in the United States, which have given extraordinary proof of the unanimity of conviction that justice has been burlesqued at Rennes." These views, says the paper, are not politically prejudiced. "...they are independent, and palpably rest on a strong and clear estimate of the latest evidence." This was probably a pointed comment aimed at the nationalist press, much of which was busy attacking British hypocrisy towards the Rennes verdict and not the verdict itself. Nevertheless, the *Irish Times* stopped short of supporting the calls of its "mainland" cousins for a boycott of the 1900 Paris exhibition.[4]

The *Irish Times* was unusual in the number of letters which appeared in the letters page on the subject, all of which were pro-Dreyfus. Whether any anti-Dreyfus ones were submitted, or whether they would have been printed, is uncertain, but the letters that did appear reflect a level of public concern that was less visible in the letters pages of most of the nationalist press.

For example, the 14th September 1899 issue carried 2 readers' letters on the subject. The first one was signed "A lover of justice", the other "A lover of truth". The first of these, which may not have been written in Ireland, advocated action and plenty of it. It suggested

> ... that public meetings be convened in all large towns; that declarations of belief in the innocence of Captain Dreyfus, and sympathy with him be taken charge of by offices and shops, and that thousands sign the "declarations"; that those lists of signatures be taken or forwarded with as little delay as possible to Madame Dreyfus; that all boards and committees forward resolutions of the same kind. Other nations may follow our example; right-thinking people in France will find their hands strengthened. ... These are only suggestions. Perhaps some one more capable may devise a more fitting way to show Captain Dreyfus that the hearts of the British people are with him.[5]

The "Lover of truth" was writing in a Dublin context, and suggested "...that an indignation meeting be held in our city in order to express our abhorrence." This writer wanted "...to have the opinion of the Dublin citizens on this matter." [6]

Four more pro-Dreyfus letters appeared in the next day's issue. Francis E. Clarke of the Rectory, Boyle, backed the idea of a league of justice and said "Let us hope that every righteous man in the land will join and swell the mighty chorus of indignation at the Rennes iniquity, which is a disgrace to modern civilisation." J. Henry Murray of Beauparc, Co. Meath said that "France has been arraigned before an impartial jury of the civilised world, and found guilty. The verdict was unanimous." Nevertheless Murray opposed a boycott, which is "...too unmanly, too mean, to be for a moment entertained by any nation that respects itself; and whatever result such action might have, it would never befriend the cause of Dreyfus."[7]

"Indignant" backed the indignation meeting idea, saying that "I hope the matter will not be allowed to drop, but that all lovers of truth and justice may put forth stringent efforts to bring about the object in view." "Materfamilias and family" said that her family and herself would gladly sign any memorial sympathising with Captain Dreyfus and his wife and family "... in the gross and cruel act of injustice under which they are suffering." [8]

Albert William Quill, a legal academic in Trinity College and author of a pro-Dreyfus poem,[9] had a letter published supporting the idea of a public meeting. He trusted "...that Dublin will not hesitate to declare its public abhorrence of the darkest and deadliest crime of the nineteenth century." Dealing with the argument against interference in another nation's affairs, Quill said that

> ...there is an implied contract between the great powers
> of Europe that none of them shall outrage our common
> humanity, and as France has trampled on all law, human
> and divine, by her cold-blooded defiance of the most el-

ementary principles of justice she must be taken to task
before the whole world.[10]

Considering the apparent strength of all this indignation, there is no record of such a public meeting ever having actually been organised or held in Dublin – unlike the
situation in Belfast, as we shall see.

The *Irish Times*, of course, represented a strain of unionism which did not reflect the sectarian divisions of a
deeply divided community in a way which would be as
characteristic of the North. A good idea of representative
Ulster unionist opinion can be gleaned from the pages of
the *Northern Whig*, a long-established Belfast daily of liberal antecedents. In August 1899, the *Whig* got huffy with
the tone of nationalist opinion on the Dreyfus trial, particularly their notion of British hypocrisy. The nationalist
papers

...do not hesitate to allege that the British Government in
Ireland has acted far more shamefully than the Dreyfus
court-martial did, and has condemned and executed innocent men as murderers in this country without any case being proved against those persons. It is shameful that such
scandalous assertions should be made. In no other country
and under no other government could they be made with
impunity.[11]

The *Whig* might be expected to have been receptive, for
sectarian reasons, to an anti-Catholic critique of the Drey-

fus affair, but it refrained from full-heartedly going down this road. However, in September 1899 there was a piece on "the philosophy of the Dreyfus case." This article paraphrased articles in the English "*National Review*" and "*The Fortnightly*" in which clericalism and Jesuitry were treated as part of the problem. *The Whig* appeared to endorse the view that "Catholicism supports the old idolatry of power, [of] blind submission to the authority of superiors"; however, the *Whig's* writer placed some hopes in the emergence of a more liberal Catholicism and did not go as far as he perhaps could have done with the anti-Catholic hypotheses.[12]

Interestingly, however, the 15th September 1899 *Whig* reported on how the Dreyfus affair came up at a meeting in Belfast of the Irish Mission to the Jews, which was a sort of Protestant "outreach" group which aimed to bring Jews around to Protestant Christianity. This meeting passed a resolution of sympathy for Madame Dreyfus, noting that "...we have followed this prosecution against your noble husband, and rejoice to know that the fruitless efforts of his enemies have failed to find any faults whatever in him, and knowing that, as we do, we are re-echoing the profoundest sentiments of the Christian public of this country." It is noteworthy that this same society later intervened on the side of the Jews in the Limerick boycott of 1904.[13] In any case, the Mission firmly linked Dreyfus's problems with Romanism, The Rev. I. Julian Grande taking the view that

… the action of the French Protestants in throwing in their lot on behalf of the martyr Captain Dreyfus had been the means of making the intelligent element of the Jewish people ponder as to its cause, and many have admitted that it was owing to the pure religion of the Reformed Christian Church.[14]

It is perhaps unsurprising that the *Whig*'s Catholic counterpart in Belfast, the nationalist *Irish News*, was less fulsomely Dreyfusard. In the earlier stages of the controversy the *News* took a vituperatively anti-Zola and anti-Semitic position,[15] but during 1899 the *News* moved towards the view that no case against Dreyfus had been proved while also, like much of the nationalist press, condemning the English press for its attacks on France, and crediting the Rennes court martial as fair by French standards.[16]

A fairly clear instance of the use of the *affaire* to promote anti-Catholic views, and thus a partial explanation of the attitude of the *News,* is evident in the letters page of the *Belfast Evening Telegraph* for 20th September 1899, about a week after the Rennes verdict. The letter was headed "The "*Irish News*" and the Dreyfus case" and signed "W.J.M."

This began:

Sir – France stands before the civilised world to-day as a melancholy example of the state of shame and degradation into which Romanism can bring an otherwise noble people. Rome has had long and undisputed sway in France ... and the pure (?) teaching of Rome has had free course among the people, and the result is that the highest in the land are sunk in infamy and corruption. The national amusement seems to be bull-fighting on Sunday and perjury and forgery the other six days. The "Irish News" is naturally ashamed of the verdict, but religious bigotry will not let it condemn the ruffians who, in the face of all evidence or want of evidence, have condemned an innocent man, and vents its spleen upon the British Press because it has denounced the unparalleled villainy of the "honourable" soldiers of France, who have only put into practical effect the teaching of their Jesuit masters, that "the end justifies the means."[17]

The correspondent gleefully contested the claim of the *Irish News* that some of the heroes of the affair such as Picquart and Labori were Catholics, and stated that they were in fact Protestants. "The perjured wretches have done their vile work, and their Jesuit teachers must feel proud of their pupils" was one of W.J.M.'s closing points.[18]

The *Belfast Newsletter's* editorial line was in most respects similar to that of the bulk of the Ulster Unionist press, but again, unlike the Southern unionist press, the *Newsletter* had no inhibitions about using the affair to attack nationalists and the Catholic Church. In their reaction to the Rennes verdict, on September 11th, the *Newsletter* declared that

The long drawn out agony of the retrial of Captain Dreyfus has ended in a calamity for France. ... No one who
has followed this melancholy farce played in the name of
justice will be surprised at the verdict. ... France in another twenty-four hours will behold herself lowered in the
estimation of the other nations. For everywhere outside her
borders the verdict will receive unanimous condemnation,
and the proceedings of the court-martial will be held up to
wonder and contempt."[19]

In their comment the next day, the *Newsletter* began
using the affair to stalk prey closer to home.

Probably no event of the century has provoked such world-
wide condemnation. ... We were almost about to say that
this view of the case was unbroken outside France, but it
is not quite; there is one exception, and we are sorry to say
that it is Ireland. The Irish Nationalist press has allowed its
hostility to Great Britain to obscure its vision, and because
the British Press has condemned the judicial crime that
France has committed, our Nationalist contemporaries
have gone the other way. The case is too gross, however,
even for Irish Nationalism to swallow completely, so we are
treated to a catalogue of palliatives and excuses, and these
are washed down with a lot of jaundiced observations about
the disgraceful way in which British hostility to France has
manifested itself during the delivery of the trial and on
the delivery of the verdict. Of course, this is all moon-
shine; there is no such thing existent as British hostility

to France; there is too much solidity in the Anglo-Saxon composition to permit of international rivalries influencing criticism of the administration of justice anywhere. ... Their [The Nationalists'] attitude now merely shows that if Ireland ever had the misfortune to come under their rule it might be possible for it to be disgraced in the eyes of the world as France now is."[20]

The next target of the *Newsletter's* Dreyfus-related opprobrium was the Church of Rome itself, which it attacked, claiming to take a cue from the London Times in a column on September 15th:

The Church of Rome all through has been an aider and abettor of the Anti-Dreyfus agitation. At the present moment the Roman Catholic Press is making the most stupendous efforts to bolster up and excuse the infamy involved in the recondemnation of Dreyfus. This effort is not confined merely to France. It is visible here in Ireland in a most flagrant manner, it is rampant in Italy under the very nose of the Vatican.[21]

The same article then set forth a conspiracy theory in which the Papacy was scheming to use the a hoped-for popular support for the French Army to bring France "back into the fold." The *Newsletter* also chose to characterise *La Croix*, the extreme anti-Semitic paper produced by the Assumptionist order, as being representative of Catholic opinion. The *Newsletter* returned to this argument on the

18th, responding at length to criticism it evidently received (from an unnamed source) of its stance.[22]

Belfast proved to outdo Dublin in actually having a public meeting on the Dreyfus issue. A display ad appeared in the *Newsletter* on the 16th September headed DREYFUS!! This advertised a public meeting at Grosvenor Hall, which featured an illustrated talk on the *affaire* given by a Mr R. Crawford Johnson, to be followed by a resolution of sympathy for Dreyfus, proposed and seconded by Mr T.P. Shillington J.P. and Alexander Taylor T.C. A lecture on the *affaire* by a Rev. D. A. De Mouilpied of Paris was also arranged for the following Tuesday at the same venue. [23]

Two days later, the *Newsletter* carried a short report of a sermon dealing with the *affaire,* given at Belmont Presbyterian Church by a Rev. J. MacDermott, taking the theme of the commandment "Thou shalt not bear false witness against thy neighbour." The reverend was reported as saying that "France had been a great nation, and it was the wish of everyone that she should again be great, but it would only be along the old lines – by men going back to God and taking His law into their hearts and lives."[24]

Further down the same page was a letter to the editor signed by a Mr A. H., who had evidently attended the well-attended Grosvenor Hall meeting. He understood that Dreyfus had been the only Jew among 200 otherwise Catholic officers.

If this is true, it is easy for your readers to understand how readily poor Dreyfus became the victim of the 199 Roman Catholic officers and the still vaster army of Jesuits and priests, who have all along done their utmost to suppress truth and righteousness and to bolster up the French army, which is now entirely in their power. Let England take warning. It is high time to awake when Ritualism and Jesuitism is corrupting the Church of England. The only analogy in history of such a dark, diabolic act is that of Dreyfus's Messiah. [25]

Derry's unionist press showed similar sympathies, with few inhibitions about making a little sectarian capital from the *affaire*. The *Londonderry Sentinel* carried a number of Items reprinted from the London *Times*, and these tended to concentrate on the supposed responsibility of Catholicism for the crisis. So, for example the item carried on September 5th 1899 and headed "The Roman Catholic Church and the Dreyfus case. Where the spy system is fostered" was attributed to that London paper. The writer, a supposed French Catholic called "Verax" blamed French clerical schooling for the paranoia which he thought had a hold on the French officer class.

I confess, Sir, that having, unfortunately, myself had personal experience of education in French schools under clerical control similar to those frequented by young Frenchmen of the class from which officers of the General Staff are mostly recruited – having, indeed, had one of the most notorious actors in the drama for a schoolfellow some thirty-five years ago- I have no hesitation in affirming that the atmosphere of those schools differs only in one degree from the atmosphere of the General Staff as revealed in the Dreyfus case. [26]

The *Sentinel's* sister unionist paper was the *Derry Standard*, which took a keenly anti-Jesuit line in its treatment of the issue. The *Standard* laid out this approach clearly in its editorial on the Rennes verdict, saying that

In this country his [Dreyfus's] acquittal was looked on as a certainty, but here the judges and the army are not under the thumb of the Jesuits, who were the real accusers and judges of Dreyfus. The Jesuits have proved their power in France, and it is all the worse for France. Dreyfus is their victim, and the success of their persecution will encourage them to further effort. [27]

The *Standard* did not pull punches in its disapproval of the nationalist attitude to the *affaire*, and indeed of nationalists in general. A few days after the Rennes verdict, the *Standard*, commenting on worldwide condemnation of the verdict, said that

It may be consoling to Dreyfus and his heroic wife to know that the whole civilised world, barring a certain section of Irish nationalists, who are only half-civilised at any rate and whose feelings are perfectly well understood, condemn the verdict as one of the greatest injustices ever committed by a legal tribunal and that has evoked universal disgust and horror. [28]

The *Standard* also dealt very bluntly with a central argument of nationalists, namely British hypocrisy in condemning the treatment of Dreyfus while practising injustice to Irish political prisoners. The *Standard's* view was simply that while the Rennes verdict was an injustice to an innocent man, a victim of the Jesuits, the militant Irish nationalist leagues and their actions "were each and all conceived in dishonesty and are evidence of a low state of morality."[29]

At the other end of the island, the unionist *Cork Constitution* also took a pro-Dreyfus line. The paper's editorial on the Rennes verdict declared that

> The French nation, or those who now control the destinies of France, have deliberately connived at the torture of an innocent man for no better reason than that the French Army may not be scandalised by bringing to book the vile conspirators who have, so far, successfully plotted and planned the ruin of Captain Dreyfus.[30]

Commenting some days later on the "extenuating circumstances" aspect of the verdict, the *Constitution* commented that "It is now being assumed that these "extenuating circumstances," involving, as they did, a recommendation to mercy, was a prearranged proceeding, meant to afford the cabinet the necessary excuse for setting this innocent victim of a foul conspiracy at liberty."[31]

Also in County Cork the *Eagle and County Cork advertiser*, which, as the *Skibbereen Eagle* had been celebrated in previous years for its quixotic warning that it had its eye on the Emperor of Russia, ran a self-parodying editorial shortly after the pardoning of Dreyfus.

> On Saturday the Eagle demanded the release of DREY-FUS. On Tuesday the President signed his pardon, and on Wednesday he was set at liberty. This was not slow work, considering that all the civilised papers had previously appealed in vain to France to give DREYFUS his freedom. Locks and bolts and bars flew open to the voice of the Eagle. Even France could not stand the piercing gaze of its eye. After this, who will deny the power of the "famous bird." DREYFUS is today a free man. Well may the Emperor of Russia live in terror while the Eagle's eye is upon him.[32]

For the robustly unionist *Carlow Sentinel*, the *affaire* reflected badly on the French people as a whole.

> What hope can there be for the future of a people of whom some three-fourths are said to approve of the conviction of a gallant officer on evidence which even their own highest court has declared to be inadequate, and on which we, in this country, would not hang a cat? The moral tone of a people which thus persists in seeing guilt where innocence is manifest, is depressed and depressing.[33]

The above passage was also carried word for word in the unionist *Meath Herald*.[34] This raises the possibility that some papers were using "off the peg" editorials, which were possibly not written locally. If so, such copy was more likely to be available to the pro-Dreyfus papers.

Another less obvious organ which rallied to the Dreyfusard cause was *Irish Society,* a fashion and gossip journal similar to *Tatler* or *Country Life,* which seldom adopted a political stance, and which is only discussed here in the "unionist" chapter because of its apparently "Castle" social affiliations. *Irish Society's* writer, in the lead up to the Rennes verdict, took the view that a politically convenient verdict would be reached in Rennes, regardless of the injustice done to the Captain. "It is not he [Dreyfus] who is on his trial but the whole of the French Army, which are represented not so much by the prisoner as by the judges themselves" said the journal before the verdict came in.[35] Afterwards, the journal declared that "The verdict may have been political, but it is certainly not just. The manner in which the Dreyfus trial was conducted shows how entirely irregular and how inequitable a French court of justice is."[36]

However, the unionist press was not entirely unanimous on the Dreyfus issue. The Dublin *Evening Mail* for one dissented from the Dreyfusard line taken by most of its cousins. Although the *Mail's* "Casual notes" column regularly made comments critical of the French anti-Dreyfusards, the *Mail's* editorial line was supportive of the Rennes Court-martial's bona fides and gave no support to the convicted officer. The *Mail* rubbished the boycott idea, and a week after the Rennes verdict the Mail commented that "When the decision was announced there was a sense-less outcry against the French nation, which was taken up in very many countries with a strange vehemence."[37] The *Mail* also printed, with evident approval, excerpts from Davitt's *Westminster Gazette* attack on the Dreyfusism of the British press. However, the *Mail* did not carry any significant anti-Semitic content.

The *Mail's* stablemate and morning counterpart, the Dublin *Daily Express*, kept up a lively debate on the affair, especially around the time of the Rennes verdict. The *Express* initially took a sceptical editorial line towards the cause of Dreyfus, but wavered significantly on this when the Rennes verdict came through. A few days before the verdict, the *Express* attacked the mainland British press for being misleading and partisan in their treatment of the Rennes Court-martial: "We cannot recall a single representative of the English press who did not go to Rennes in the strong belief that Dreyfus is innocent, and who has not coloured with that belief everything that he has since written about this trial."[38]

Nevertheless, the *Express* did find its sympathies lying more with the accused after the verdict:

> We have striven throught this terrible trial … to maintain a judicial reserve, and, as our readers are aware, we were prepared, and strove to prepare them, for a verdict adverse to the prisoner; but we confess the news of that sentence on Saturday has come upon us with a painful shock.[39]

The same editorial admitted that the paper's sentiment "has grown of late much stronger than it used to be in favour of his innocence."[40]

All the same, the *Express* repeatedly asked its readers to look at the case from the point of view of the military judges, who had a difficult task, and to bear in mind that there was still apparently some circumstantial evidence against Dreyfus. This was the perspective taken in a 3-part study of the case by a J. F. Taylor, whose articles were headed "Some thoughts on the Dreyfus case. By an Irish Q.C." published on the 16th, 23rd and 30th of September.

In these articles, Taylor put the evidential case against Dreyfus as the French prosecutors might have seen it. Taylor made much of the "Mulhausen incident" by which was meant Dreyfus's trip in 1894 to his birthplace of Mulhausen (Mulhouse) in occupied Alsace around the time that German military manoeuvres were being held there, which was consistent with the writer of the *bordereau* mentioning to his German paymasters that he was going to be present at manoeuvres.[41]Taylor considered Dreyfus's "secretive character" significant,[42] and also defended the opinions of the handwriting analyst and criminologist Bertillon, who had found Dreyfus to be the writer of the bordereau.[43]

Taylor's column of the 16th was the subject of a short but vigorous critique by the British theologian and noted Dreyfusard commentator, F. C. Conybeare, who accused Taylor of turning a blind eye to major Henry's perjury, and lacking in "fairness or integrity" in his discussion of Henry.[44] Nevertheless, Taylor stuck to his argument, saying that "...I submit in justice to the French officers that there was a great deal to make them look with suspicion on Dreyfus, whose bearing at the trial seems to have disillusioned many others besides Mr W. Steevens and Mr Murray Gibbon."[45]

The *Express* also published several letters on the affair at the time of Rennes, On September 14th, the paper carried a letter from a W. F. P. Stockley (address not given) referring with favour to a letter from the French Jesuit Provincial opposing anti-Semitism, and one from a Walter Sweetman of Ferns criticising Dreyfus's defence team for not sufficiently rebutting the argument of the "Mulhausen incident."[46] There were a number of other letters discussing the ins and outs of the Mulhausen incident, and a couple asking about the pronunciation of Dreyfus[47], but there were none which expressed the simple outrage of those in the *Irish Times*.

Overall, however, unionist papers took an almost uniformly pro-Dreyfus position, but not necessarily for the usual liberal Dreyfusard reasons. The *Irish Times* followed something like an Anglo-Saxon liberal agenda, stressing the concept of justice to an individual. However, the tone of Ulster unionist papers was different, being much more one of complacent satisfaction in the superiority of British and Protestant ways, combined with a preparedness to contrast these with benighted Romanism and Nationalism.

Endnotes

1 Dublin was the *Times's* second largest circulation centre. See Davison, N.R. *James Joyce, Ulysses and the construction of Jewish identity* (Cambridge University Press, 1996) p.66. Joyce apparently considered the *Times* as having more accurate reporting of the case than its Irish counterparts.

2 *Irish Times,* 15th February 1898

3 *Irish Times,* 26th February 1898

4 *Irish Times*, 13th September 1899

5 *Irish Times,* 14th September 1899

6 Ibid.

7 *Irish Times,* 15th September 1899

8 Ibid.

9 *Irish Times,* 30th August 1899

10 *Irish Times*, 19th September 1899

11 *Northern Whig,* 8th August 1899

12 *Northern Whig,* 2nd September 1899

13 See Keogh, Dermot and McCarthy, Andrew, *Limerick Boycott 1904: anti-Semitism in Ireland* (Cork: Mercier Press, 2005) p.91

14 *Northern Whig*, 15th September 1899

15 For instance see *Irish News,* 15th February 1898

16 For example, *Irish News,* 13th September 1899. See also chapter on provincial nationalist press below.

17 *Belfast Evening Telegraph,* 20th September 1899

18 Ibid.

19 *Belfast Newsletter,* 11th September 1899

20 *Belfast Newsletter,* 12th September 1899

21 *Belfast Newsletter,* 15th September 1899

22 *Belfast Newsletter,* 18th September 1899

23 *Belfast Newsletter,* 16th September 1899. This meeting, according to the Dublin *Daily Express* attracted 3000 people and reported one speaker as saying that "They thanked God they were members of the British Constitution, under which every man got a fair trial." (*Daily Express* (Dublin) 18 September 1899).

24 *Belfast Newsletter,* 18th September 1899

25 Ibid.

26 *Londonderry Sentinel,* 5th September 1899

27 *Derry Standard,* 11th September 1899

28 *Derry Standard,* 13th September 1899

29 *Derry Standard,* 22nd September 1899

30 *Cork Constitution,* 12rh September 1899

31 *Cork Constitution,* 21st September 1899

32 *Eagle and County Cork advertiser,* 23rd September 1899

33 *Carlow Sentinel,* 16th September 1899

34 *Meath Herald,* 16th September 1899

35 *Irish Society,* 9th September 1899

36 *Irish Society,* 16th September 1899

37 *Dublin Evening Mail,* 20th September 1899

38 *Daily Express* (Dublin), 8th September 1899

39 *Daily Express* (Dublin), 11th September 1899

40 Ibid

41 *Daily Express* (Dublin), 23rd September 1899

42 Ibid.

43 *Daily Express* (Dublin), 30th September 1899

44 *Daily Express* (Dublin), 23rd September 1899

45 *Daily Express* (Dublin), 23rd September 1899

46 Both these letters are in *Daily Express* (Dublin), 14th September 1899

47 For example see *Daily Express* (Dublin), 15th September 1899

THE CATHOLIC PRESS

Writers in Irish Catholic periodicals would certainly have been aware of events and currents of opinion in Catholic Europe, especially France, the "eldest daughter of the Church." The French Church in the 1890s was in a much more conciliatory position towards the Republic than it would have been 2 decades earlier. The relationship between the Catholic Church and the French Republic had evolved significantly since the crises of the 1870's, and there was no longer such a clear dichotomy between anti-clerical republicans on the one hand and Catholic anti-republicans on the other. Pope Leo XIII had become reconciled to the French Republic, and the tone of his leadership of the Church in the world of the 1890s was set by his encyclical *Rerum Novarum* (1891) which set out the parameters of a Catholic social policy.

The *"Ralliement,"* the name given to this pro-republican reconciliation was, simultaneously, a call on French Catholics to accept and adhere to the Republic, and to influence the Republic's politics in a way that would counter the secularising tendencies of radical republicanism. However, this point of view did not necessarily reflect the preference of French conservatives, many of whose hearts were still Royalist. Anti-Semitism, though actively discouraged by Pope Leo XIII[1], had its Catholic and clerical supporters. In France, the most notable of these was the Assumptionist order, publishers of the very widely read (and very anti-Semitic) paper, *La Croix*. Catholic anti-Semitism was also strong in Austria, where Vienna Mayor Karl Lueger's Christian Social movement espoused it, and elsewhere in Europe, though it was much weaker among Anglophone Catholics.

Irish Catholic religious periodicals varied considerably with regard to readership and therefore tone. Some, such as the *Irish Rosary,* were aimed at a devotional lay readership, and others like the *Lyceum* and its successor the *New Ireland Review* were tailored towards the Catholic intelligentsia and clergy. The *Irish Ecclesiastical Record* was the only journal published under anything like direct supervision of the Hierarchy. Most of these journals commented only sparingly on public affairs.

An exception to this, and a good indicator of conservative Catholic opinion on public issues at the time, is the *Irish Catholic* which, while not an official Church mouthpiece, was a reliable conduit for opinions that would be considered acceptable to the Church. The *Irish Catholic's* writers would have been fully cognizant of Church policy toward France, including acceptance of republican institutions, combined with opposition to secularist laicisation.

Commenting on the *affaire* in January 1898, at the time of the Esterhazy acquittal, the paper stated that "In the condemnation of Dreyfus the whole body of circumcised aliens was struck a deadly blow, and since then they have fallen from their position of public masters and have been forced, in some degree, into the political Ghetto from which they should never have been allowed to issue." The same piece continued:

> The Jews are utterly discredited and routed in every quarter; nothing that can possibly happen in the interval can cleanse them of the terrible stains left on their name by the Dreyfus and Panama scandals. Their one force is money, but money does not of itself assume a personality, and there are now no men of note to represent Hebrew finance before the popular tribunal.[2]

The paper said that the Dreyfus and Panama scandals marked a loss of power for France's Masonic-Jewish elite and was an opportunity for the Republic (which the paper, following the official Church line, accepted) to come under the control of Catholic statesmen, exemplified by Albert de Mun or the Duc D'Aumale.[3]

Although in February 1898 the paper alleged that the magnificent achievements of Catholic France at home and abroad were being deliberately undermined, indeed persecuted, by the policies of "a government of Jews, Freemasons and Atheists,"[4] The markedly anti-Semitic content of earlier editorials started to be toned down, possibly as a result of ecclesiastical pressure. During 1899 the paper posited a distinction between sincere and malicious Dreyfusards, for example in August 1899, when it commented that

> A wide gulf ... exists between those whom we may style

the honest defenders of Dreyfus, and those who only advocate his cause because it has seemed to them to provide a fulcrum on which to rest the Socialist and Anarchist levers which are being employed for the disruption of the edifices of society, and of the State. [5]

At the time of the Rennes verdict, the paper defended the court-martial's bona fides without mentioning the Jews,[6] and in December the paper acknowledged that anti-Semitic writings such as those of Drumont

"... circulated amongst an excitable people, are eminently calculated to produce a dangerous situation, from which might easily flow events fraught with blood-shed and disgrace." Significantly, the paper repudiated the blood libel, the idea that Jews drank the blood of Christian Children, in quite strong terms: "There is absolutely nothing in the ritual or practices of the Judaic religion which affords even the most remote foundation for the gross and horrible legend which involves atrocious libel on a people so many of whom were amongst the first members of the Christian Church."[7]

However, this did not make the Jews blameless. The same article also declared:

We are far from adopting or holding the view that no share of blame attaches to the Jews themselves for the feeling of ill-will towards them, which is widespread amongst French Catholics. The sentiment of enmity in question is, no doubt, in large measure, based on economic causes, and on resentment produced by the financial exactions of Hebrew usurers.[8]

Added to this was the fact that many Jewish politicians "have been openly avowed and unrelenting enemies of the Church, of the Christian religion, and of its sacerdotal and cloistered servants." In effect, "The Jew in France has deliberately and needlessly made himself the agent of a pagan persecution of the Church, his participation in which in large degree tends to explain the hostility with which he is regarded by many Catholics." The editorial concluded that "We have very little doubt that if, for example, the Jewish legislators of France were to exhibit less hatred of Christianity than they now display, the entire situation in that country would soon undergo a vast and salutary change." [9]

That the *Irish Catholic*'s views were within the folds of Catholic acceptability does not mean that they were typical of lay or even clerical Catholic opinion at the time, but there are not many instances from Irish Catholic periodicals where any very different views were expressed. The main Catholic intelligentsia journal in Ireland at this time was the *New Ireland Review*, a successor to the *Lyceum*, in which a Fr. Finlay had published a piece in 1893 had warned against allowing Jewish immigration to Ireland.[10] *New Ireland Review* had a piece in April 1899 signed by "Manvelly" which seemed to endorse the view that the need to uphold the honour of the French Army must outweigh justice to an individual, and that anyone taking the

Army's oath must be prepared to accept this. Manvelly argued that

> An insult to the Army is an insult to every Frenchman. Every attempt to undermine his faith in it has but the effect of inflaming it. ... Add to this that the culprit belongs to a religion, or rather to a race, which the immense majority of Frenchman detest, and one begins to realise the intensity of the passions aroused by the double insult to the national honour.[11]

On the other hand, an earlier issue of the same journal, from the period of the Zola trial, carried a piece by a J. Mordant, called "The Zola-Dreyfus mystery" which took a much more critical view of Official France's behaviour. The author commented that "If one thing is clear out of all this chaos, it is that the [French] Government and the War Office have been engaged in an unholy conspiracy to defeat the ends of justice. They have stood loyally together, lying, deceiving, terrorising, victimising through thick and thin."[12]

There was one pronouncement from a senior Irish Catholic Churchman touching on the *affaire*. The *Daily Nation* of 27th September 1899 was one of several newspapers which carried the text of a short letter from Cardinal Logue, to an un-named recipient, in which he said it was pointless in the existing climate to express any definite opinion. Logue commented:

Even were I in a position to form an opinion, I would think it useless to give expression to it. It is a hopeless task to attempt to reason with or impress madmen; and an amount of madness has developed on this question among English writers and English speakers which time, and perhaps the cold weather, may alleviate, but which facts, or reasoning on facts, would only aggravate.[13]

The Cardinal's statement of apparent reluctance to give an opinion, however, says quite a lot in itself. For Logue, the "madness" of the controversy lay with the body of English opinion, not French. The tone of Logue's letter was in some contrast to that of his English counterpart Cardinal Vaughan, who defended the French Church from accusations made against it, but who also expressed himself in sympathy with the judgement of his countrymen. Vaughan's letter to the Times, dated 17 September 1899, said "It is unjust to identify the Catholic Church with the act of injustice whereby Dreyfus was condemned at Rennes without clear evidence of guilt."[14]

In any case, Logue did have one other thing to say which came close to the subject, though not to the press, and he said it in a letter to Archbishop Walsh of Dublin which he wrote on 22nd December 1899. In this letter, Logue decided to make a passing remark about a section of the English Catholic press.

I don't know whether Your Grace has noticed the line which has been taken and the tone of the so called English

Catholic papers, such as the "New Era", and sometimes even the "Catholic Times" is not far from it. I have seen only one number of the "Weekly Register" and have found this tendency strong in it. They seem to regard themselves as having a mission to combat the Catholic press of the continent and to advocate the cause of the Jews, who are certainly the bitterest opponents of the Church in France and Italy. It often occurs to me that we are hardly justified in permitting these papers to circulate among our people as Catholic without a word to warn the unwary of their true character.[15]

Walsh's views on the *affaire* are not known, but his first biographer does mention that "When the Dreyfus *affaire* was at its height, the Archbishop, who happened to be in France at the time, acquired a singularly accurate knowledge of the details of that intricate case. Later, he keenly enjoyed reading Mr Dooley's humorous presentation of the same *affaire*, beginning "J'accuse" says Zola, "and they thrun him out." " [16]

The Catholic hierarchy may not have been of one mind on events in France at that time. A possibly different view of the affair was hinted at in a sermon given by Dr Lyster, the Bishop of Achonry at the opening of a Mercy convent school in Sligo, which was reproduced in full in the *Sligo Champion*. Lyster was attacking the continental system of "godless" secular education, during which theme he turned his attention to France:

Cast your gaze on France, once the glory of the Catholic
world, the eldest daughter of the Church – the land which
Clovis won by his victories, which Clotilde gained by her
prayer, the birthplace of Joan of Arc, the home of Vincent
de Paul, where good St Louis reigned, the country blessed
by the miracle of Lourdes, sanctified by the vision of the
Sacred Heart – shaken, riven, torn by shock after shock of
successive revolution, until we see her to-day the bye-word
of the nations – trying to save her sense of justice from being a travesty, and her army from being her shame – where
since last Sunday's sun went down the revolting orgies of
the Revolution have been revived, the abomination of des-
olation has been again in the holy place; savage hands have
pulled down the emblem of God the crucified; brutal feet
have trodden upon the Abiding Presence of God himself.
And this – the out come of her godless schools.[17]

The above passage is by no means an episcopal endorsement of the Dreyfusard cause, but, in the reference to "trying to save her sense of justice from being a travesty," it
does have echoes of the Catholic Dreyfusardism that was
made explicit in the *Kilkenny Journal*.

Other Irish Catholic publications of the period, whether
or not they mentioned the *affaire*, were quite consistent in
portraying the Church in France in the role of a persecuted entity. For example, Catholic Truth Society of Ireland
pamphlets put much of the blame for the state of affairs in
France on Freemasonry,[18] but did not link this to Jews or to
the Dreyfus affair. This pattern is also visible in the quasi-

official *Irish Ecclesiastical Record*. The *Record* carried no mention of the Dreyfus affair in 1898-99 or indeed for the years immediately following, but it did carry a number of pieces on Freemasonry which exemplify the considerable hostility directed against that craft by the Church at this time. Indeed, a high proportion of the record's comment on foreign events was taken up by these attacks on Freemasonry, and it is reasonable to suppose that this was a code through which the *Record's* writers portrayed events in much of the world.

In 1899, a C. M. O'Brien wrote a piece on Freemasonry in which he outlined the Church's opposition to it, and gave details of its rituals. A large part of the article then detailed the support of Masonry for France's revolutions of 1789 and 1848, their ultimate motive for this being the extirpation of Catholicism. However, having taken the reader up to the 1890s, the writer then finished the piece by saying that Masonry had entered a period of decline. This is particularly curious given the state of affairs in France at that point, and suggests an almost explicit reluctance on the part of the author to comment on the situation then current in France.[19] The same volume of the *Record* carried items on Masonic assaults on the Church in Latin America and in Mexico in particular.[20] Similarly, an item in the Dominicans' *Irish Rosary* blamed Freemasonry for Spain's loss of the Philippines.[21]

The theme which ran alongside this concern with Freemasonry was that of persecution of the Church, throught the Catholic world but especially in France. Some articles in the Catholic press detailed the banefulness of French secularism, without discussing the context in which the secular movement had gained strength. In 1900, C. M. O'Brien wrote in the *Record* under the title "The modern reign of terror in France" about the anti-clericals' ascendancy in that country. He observed that "The gigantic Tour Eiffel commemorates the bloody revolution of 1789, which ended in the reign of terror" and went on to lament the political weakness of contemporary French Catholicity, attributing this to lack of political leadership. The answer was for the Catholic laity to organise. "Truly if the laity could be roused to a sense of their duty and their power, they could, at a single blow, drive every atheist, Freemason, and Jew, from the Chamber and the Senate"[22]

Such articles about the Freemasons and the Laicising movement in France were significant not least because of what they did not say. There was no attempt made in the *Record* to acknowledge, much less meet, criticism levelled by liberals at the Church in France, for example on the anti-Semitic campaign of the Assumptionist order through their paper *La Croix*, but instead only bitter complaints about secularist persecution, devoid of the context which discussion of the Dreyfus controversy would have supplied. There was, therefore, almost certainly a deliberate policy in the *Record* of not mentioning the *affaire*.

Overall, the attitudes expressed in the Catholic press would suggest a greater receptiveness in the Irish Church to currents of opinion on the continent than to those that were usual in Britain. We see no willingness at all in Irish

Catholic papers to echo the liberal attitude of Cardinal Vaughan in England. Instead, Irish publications seemingly chose to share the sense of persecution being felt or expressed in France. It should be said in balance to this that there really were Church desecrations happening in France at this time, and that Catholics not opposed to Dreyfus (vide Bishop Lyster or the *Kilkenny Journal*) were as repelled by this as anyone writing in the *Record*.

In any event, there is also no doubt that there was a discernible tone of anti-Semitism in Irish Catholic papers. This anti-Semitism was not as extreme as, for example, that of *United Irishman*, and it must also be said that there was clear opposition to the blood-libel stigma, and that no support was given to introducing measures against Jews. However, French Jews were consistently portrayed as enemies of the Church. Cardinal Logue clearly saw them as such, and we also see this view exemplified in the *Irish Catholic's* statement that "The Jew in France has deliberately and needlessly made himself the agent of a pagan persecution of the Church, his participation in which in large degree tends to explain the hostility with which he is regarded by many Catholics." In other words, The Jew was an enemy not because of his race, but principally because he was the deliberate ally of the laicisers and a willing participant in the secularist reign of terror.[23]

Endnotes

1 For example, Leo's dressing down of Bailly (editor of *la Croix*). See Larkin, Maurice *Church and state after the Dreyfus affair: the separation issue in France* (Macmillan 1974) p.79.

2 *Irish Catholic*, January 22nd 1898

3 *Irish Catholic,* January 29th 1898

4 *Irish Catholic*, 12th February 1898

5 *Irish Catholic*, 26th August 1899

6 *Irish Catholic*, 16th September 1899

7 *Irish Catholic*, 2nd December 1899

8 Ibid.

9 Ibid.

10 *Lyceum*, July 1893

11 *New Ireland Review*, April 1899

12 *New Ireland Review*, May 1898

13 Quoted in *Daily Nation*, 27thSeptember 1899

14 *Times* (London) 17 September 1899, carried in *Irish Catholic,* 23rd September 1899

15 Logue to Walsh, 22nd December 1899 (in Dublin Diocesan Archives). Underlining in original.

16 Walsh, Patrick J. *William J. Walsh: Archbishop of Dublin* (Cork:Talbot press, 1927) p.581. The "Mr Dooley" sketch was one of many written by the American humourist Finley Peter Dunne.

17 *Sligo Champion*, 26th August 1899

18 For instance Bellingham, Henry *Freemasonry and the Church in France*, Catholic Truth Society of Ireland pamphlet no 473, 1913

19 *Irish Ecclesiastical Record*, vol. .vi (July-December 1899) p.325

20 Ibid, p.35 and p.267

21 *Irish Rosary*, February1899 p.105

22 *Irish Ecclesiastical Record*, vol. .viii, (July-December 1900), p.265.

23 As a final footnote, it may also be worth mentioning that the work of one Irish Clerical novelist, Canon Sheehan, has been remarked on for linking Jewry and Masonry with Fenianism. See discussion of Sheehan's novel *My new curate* (1898) in R. Fleischmann *Catholic nationalism in the Irish revival: a study of Canon Sheehan, 1852-1913* (Macmillan 1997) p.51

Irish anti-Dreyfusards (3)
Michael Davitt believed Jewish power underlay the campaign to
free Dreyfus.
(With permission of National Library of Ireland)

The expatriate Irish press

Irish emigrant communities were well established in a number of countries by the late 1890s. The largest were in Britain and the United States, but Australia, Canada and even Argentina also had sizeable communities. However, not all of these expatriate populations were served by a press of their own at that time. The US and Argentina had Irish papers of a Catholic and nationalist hue, but Britain at this time had none.

In Canada and Australia, Irish Catholic opinion could be discerned in the Catholic Press, but again no specifically Irish newspaper was in business.

Nevertheless, those newspapers that were published by or for Irish communities outside Ireland offer some potential for interesting insights into Irish opinions on the *affaire*. On one hand, Irish journalists abroad were more likely than at home to find a Dreyfusard climate of opinion around them, particularly in Anglophone countries. On the other hand, they were also quite likely to assert an Irish nationalist perspective, possibly in reaction to that.

An interesting example of these twin pressures can be found in Argentina, which had a large and influential first and second generation Irish community by the 1890s. They were served by the Buenos Aires *Southern Cross*, a pro-nationalist weekly paper. The stance taken by the *Southern Cross* incorporated elements both of pro-Dreyfus world opinion and the critique of British cant and hypocrisy that we have seen in Dublin's nationalist press.

In August 1899, on foot of the attempted assassination of Dreyfus's lawyer Labori, the *Southern Cross* stated that

> That Dreyfus is innocent is recognised by 90% of the people of France. The transparent perjury of his accusers is shown in every detail of the trial and only those who wilfully close their eyes to the facts can still range themselves against the unfortunate victim of the General Staff.

However, the same article combined this view with a defence of France against what the editor presumably saw as anti-French prejudice.

> Those who blame France for the Dreyfus case ... know not what they say. It is because France – the justice loving frank and kindly people of France – bear no blame for Dreyfus that he is being returned to Rennes. ... Many greater crimes are unrecorded in recent history. The Dreyfus wrong is possible under any government in Europe, but perhaps its exposure is not possible in any country but France.[1]

This defence of the good faith of the French people, presumably from attack by those who condemned France as a whole for the treatment of Dreyfus, was a pattern in Irish nationalist discussion of the *affaire* at this stage, but the

Southern Cross did not share the line of some nationalists, who went on to defend the bona-fides of the court-martial. The *Southern Cross* did, however, take up the other nationalist theme, the attack on the hypocrisy of foreign critics of France. In late August 1899, the *Southern Cross* developed its anti-hypocrisy argument, asking critics of France to

> … look to Ireland and to English rule there. Let them examine the records of Dublin Castle, from the Treaty of Limerick to the close of the Rebellion of '98 and, thick as are the graves of martyred patriots on Irish soil, will they find unpublished instances of perfidy which overshadow the Dreyfus wrong and cause it to look half-hearted and insignificant.[2]

The view of the *Southern Cross* on the Rennes verdict were a restatement of its editorial line which supported the innocence of Dreyfus, but also upheld the good faith of the French public, let down by a military clique, and decried the hypocrisy which they saw in international condemnations of the verdict.

> Dreyfus has been re-convicted but in such a manner as to establish his innocence of the charges brought against him. The military tribunal before which his case was heard was not in a position to judge him impartially and consequently time has been lost. Revision must come of course, or pardon. It is a question between the military clique and public opinion…Meanwhile we think that half

the protests we hear on all sides are the merest hypocrisy – the most contemptible cant. … We hear of protests from the United States formulated by men who have not rushed into the streets to call for world-wide obloquy of the roasters of niggers condemned to a death of fire without trial. … We hear of protests in Buenos Aires by Argentine students, who had not a single reproach to throw at the court which decided on the Rosales' case, and which his the tragedy of that terrible event from the light of day. We hear that the Pharisees protest; and the pirates, the land-grabbers, the rapers, the tricksters, the wreckers take up the chorus. It is the old story. They have not a clean hand amongst them all, yet they throw the stone.[3]

As it happens, a regular contributor to, and future editor of, the *Southern Cross* at this time was the local Irish resident William Bulfin who, a few years later wrote *Rambles in Éirinn*, an account of people he met while journeying around Ireland. These musings included what has been described as a "nasty, anti-Semitic depiction" of a Jewish pedlar.[4]

The United States had an extensive Irish press. One paper which consciously brought together Irish and Catholic perspectives was the Boston *Pilot*, founded in the 1830s by, and still at this time published by, Patrick Donahoe. The *Pilot*, like its Southern hemisphere counterpart the *Southern Cross*, took a line which both upheld the innocence of Dreyfus and condemned what it saw as the hypocrisy of sections of international opinion.

The *Pilots's* instincts were not particularly advanced or liberal. During the Zola trial, which arose from *J'accuse*, the *Pilot* had this to say:

> Zola made a bold defence, and he may be innocent or he may be guilty; but as between him and his antagonists, the honours of decency are on their side. Zola's published works prove him to be a man who delights in sensationalism, and cares not how dirty the means by which he may achieve it. [5]

At around this time, the *Pilot* felt it necessary to comment on the subject of persecution of the Jews, and to dissociate this practice from Catholicism.

> It is true that in France and Italy the Jews wield an influence out of all proportion to their numbers. It is also true that this influence is usually unfriendly to the Church. But neither of these facts can make it lawful to persecute those who honestly believe in Judaism, and that they so believe we must assume unless the contrary is proved. [6]

In late Summer 1899, as the Rennes court-martial neared its end, The *Pilot* carried a lengthy article by a Joseph Smith, who took the common Catholic line that Dreyfus was the victim of a military clique, that France as a nation was better able than others to deal with injustice, and that Anglo-Saxon attacks on that nation were cant. Smith said of the indignant Anglo-Saxons:

They care little for Dreyfus or his cause; they care much for their prejudices against France and the French. As they cudgel France with Dreyfus, they call complacently to the world: "now do you not see the superiority of the grand old Anglo-Saxon over the decaying Latin and the excitable Celt? "

Dreyfus, said Smith, was the victim of a

... gang of Jew-baiters, royalists, forgers and conspirators who are strenuously seeking to wreck the French republic. However, "The fact that France, in the teeth of dangers that threaten her political existence, is striving hard to correct a judicial military crime appears to have no weight whatever with the British and American Pharisee.

Smith's article went on to point out that Catholic France, unlike Prussia and Russia, allowed Jews to serve as officers, and that in England there would be no Dreyfus affair because Dreyfus would have been executed.[7]

The *Pilot* felt forced to re-state its case for the French sense of Justice after the Rennes verdict was announced. The paper denied that Dreyfus's Jewishness was the main cause of the situation that had developed. The *Pilot* also referred to the new verdict as "cowardly and cruel" and said that the honour of the French Army was only being saved "... at the expense of natural honesty and justice." The editorial continued:

... it appears pretty evident that Dreyfus is not sacrificed because he is a Jew, but because the army needs a scapegoat, and picked him out as the most convenient victim. ... But alas, it is not the military ring, but France herself, that will suffer from this atrocious miscarriage of justice, unless the Government have the courage to defy the army and reopen the case.

The editorial finally placed its trust in the President, who was a plain country-man, and "The country people are honest, virtuous, thrifty. They believe in God and his justice; and without them, France would indeed be doomed."[8]

The New York *Irish American* was another strongly Catholic and pro-nationalist paper which expressed views similar to those of the *Pilot*. In the aftermath of the Rennes Verdict, the *Irish American* carried the statement of the highly influential (and Irish-born) Archbishop John Ireland of St Paul, Minnesota on how Catholics might respond to the verdict and to the vehemence of protests in the US. Ireland referred to the anti-Rennes protests as being "... untimely, unfair to France, and likely to breed a regrettable ill-feeling between that country and our own." Ireland's statement cast cold water on the feelings behind those protests, but did not go as far as to defend the French Army or the Rennes verdict itself

I can well understand and explain the present happenings in America. The American people are most easily roused to sentiments of justice and humanity. An appeal to such sentiments thrills and moves them to almost instantaneous action, often without time being taken to consider whether such an action is timely, or whether even the appeal, made in the name of justice and humanity, is one really and substantially founded on fact.[9]

However, about a fortnight after the Rennes verdict, when Dreyfus received a pardon from President Loubet, the *Irish American* carried a more forthright comment on what had happened:

Captain Dreyfus, the innocent victim of the intrigue of a wretched clique in the headquarters staff of the French Army, has been liberated, by direction of the President of the Republic, in order to prevent the trial of an appeal against the unjust verdict by which he was condemned, and General Gallifet, the Minister of Military Affairs, has officially declared that "The Dreyfus incident has been finally closed." The Minister is in error, as he will find out ere long. No "incident" is ever finally closed by any decision by which truth and justice are equally outraged. Sooner or later the right will be vindicated; and then the condemnation of those who are really guilty will be all the heavier the longer it is delayed. [10]

The other major New-York Irish paper was the *Irish World*, edited by Patrick Ford. This extremely forthright and opinionated journal lost few opportunities to attack anything which smacked of imperialism or Anglo-Saxon-ism. For example, regarding US involvement in the Philippines, the *Irish World* took the view that imperialism and a sense of Anglo-Saxon superiority had combined in trying to justify the subjugation of the Filipino people.[11]

The *Irish World* carried mostly American and Irish news and comment, but also took an Anti-British stance where possible, such as on the Boer war.[12] It seldom commented on issues not directly relevant to the US, Ireland or Britain, and there was little or no mention of the Dreyfus affair during 1898 and most of 1899. Considering the opportunities that existed for Irish nationalist publications to denounce the hypocrisy of British attacks on a French injustice, the lack of comment in the *Irish World* can be seen as strangely reticent.

However, not long after the Rennes verdict, the *Irish World* carried a forthright piece written by the progressive, Irish-born Presbyterian educator and clergyman Robert Ellis Thompson. Thompson's piece was well attuned to the *Irish World's* anti-imperialist and anti-militarist agenda. His thesis was that the injustice done to Dreyfus was symptomatic of a country given over to militarism, which is where he thought America was also headed.

The preposterous verdict of the military court at Rennes, which has called out the reprobation of all Christendom, is no isolated fact, without its warnings for the civilized nations. ... Let no country set itself up against France in Pharasaic conceit, as though she were a sinner in ways beyond our imitation. The iniquity of this sentence grows out of a folly which every great nation in Christendom shares with her, and which we are cherishing at this moment more than any other of our number. That folly is militarism.[13]

Thompson's analysis of the situation in France went on to argue that her history of conscription had led to the despotism of Napoleon, and that later, the defeat of 1871, the demand for *revanche* against Germany and the unpopularity of the Third Republic's politicians had all conspired to produce an exaggerated deference to the army. In this situation, mistakes and injustices had to be covered up. "That he [Dreyfus] was a scapegoat to hide the guilt of others was a small matter. That a revision of his case was sure to produce a scandal, and to put the army in a bad light before the world, was reason enough to stop any such procedure." The state of affairs of which the Dreyfus case was symptomatic, said Thompson, was also on its way to America.

Once the American people make up their mind that they have a mission to improve the rest of mankind by bayonets and bullets, we are entered upon a very large field of operations, and we shall pass insensibly from stage to stage in the career, as Rome did, as did England, as did every great empire that was not the creation of an individual ambition. The day for a universal conscription of our citizens is not far off, and when it comes the army will be the real ruler of the nation, and the authority of its generals will outweigh that of its congresses and presidents, long before it finds it necessary to supersede them.[14]

Australia was one area where Irish Catholic and nationalist perspectives were aired via the Catholic Press. Catholic periodicals in Australia were conduits for anti-Dreyfus stories,[15] and Irish perspectives were added to this. There was a marked tinge of "what about the Irish" in some of the Catholic press discussion of the *affaire*. One of the most prominent providers of such views was Michael Davitt, who wrote in the *Advocate* that England was showing hypocrisy and cant, calling for justice to be done to Dreyfus while inflicting much worse injustices against South Africa. Davitt also alleged that the enormous financial power of the Jews had been turned against France because of economic ties to anti-Semitic Russia.[16] A J. P. Brennan argued in the Catholic journal *Austral Light* that British eloquence on Dreyfus' behalf was, given their treatment of Davitt and other Irish political prisoners, merely "feigned indignation and claptrap eloquence."[17]

The Sydney *Freeman's Journal* was, in terms of content, a Catholic Journal first and an Irish Journal second. Its comments on the Rennes verdict emphasized shock at the verdict one week, and a spirited attack on what they saw as over-reaction to that verdict the next. Just after the verdict, the *Journal* expressed alarm at the possible threat posed to democracy by the verdict: "When an army can so impress a court-martial as to cause that body to give a decision flat in the face of evidence, it will not be long before that army is the master of France under some tyrannical dictator."[18] A week later, however, the *Journal* turned its fire on the reaction to the verdict in the Anglo-Saxon world:

> In their hysterical anger at the verdict they clamour that France should be punished, that she should be boycotted, that her exhibition should be ruined; and senseless injustice has been done to Frenchmen abroad by hysterical employ-ers both in England and America, who seek to equalize the supposed injustice done to Dreyfus by "sacking" any of his countrymen who may be in her employ.[19]

The *Journal* went on to remark cuttingly on anti-Catho-lic conspiracy theories: "The silliest accusation arising out of the Rennes verdict is that it is the result of Roman Cath-olic intrigue. For this charge there is not enough evidence to satisfy even a Sydney Orangeman."[20]

The expatriate press commentary on the *affaire* has ech-oes of a "Catholic Dreyfusardism" which can also be seen in parts of the Irish nationalist press, markedly more in provincial Ireland than in Dublin. This position was one which asserted the innocence of Dreyfus not from a liberal or secularist point of view, but one which defended the Catholic Church and the people of France, with the blame for the *affaire* being placed on militarism or even godless-ness. The context in which the expatriate press operated was different, but not so different that views similar to those of the *Irish Catholic* or even the *United Irishman* could not have been expressed if desired.

Endnotes

1 *Southern Cross*, 18th August 1899.

2 *Southern Cross*, 25th August 1899

3 *Southern Cross*, 15th September 1899.

4 See O'Grada, *Jews in Ireland in the age of Joyce: a socioeconomic history* (Princeton University Press, 2006) p.180.

5 *Pilot* (Boston), 5th March 1898.

6 *Pilot* (Boston), 19th March 1898

7 *Pilot* (Boston), 2nd September 1899

8 *Pilot* (Boston), 16th September 1899

9 *Irish American*, 16th September 1899

10 *Irish American*, 23rd September 1899

11 *Irish World*, 7th January 1899

12 For example see *Irish World*, 16th August 1899

13 *Irish World*, 23rd September 1899

14 Ibid.

15 See Thornton-Smith, Colin Reactions of the Australian Catholic press to the Dreyfus case in *Australian Jewish Historical Society Journal*, 1997, 14/57 (p.57-92).

16 *Advocate,* 28th October 1899, as summarised in Thornton-Smith, op cit. p.74.

17 *Austral Light*, October 1899, as summarised in Thornton-Smith op cit. p.75

18 *Freeman's Journal* (Sydney), 16th September 1899

19 *Freeman's Journal* (Sydney), 23rd September 1899

20 Ibid.

Irish anti-Dreyfusards (4)
Frank Hugh O'Donnell was the most extreme Irish anti-Semite
writing in this period.
(With permission of National Library of Ireland)

THE VIEWS OF IRISH INTELLECTUALS –
A FOOTNOTE

The Dreyfus controversy in France was a cause célèbre for intellectuals, and as such it undoubtedly played a part in the development of the 20th century's liberal and human rights philosophies. It has even been plausibly argued that "intellectuals" were first defined as a group by the *affaire.*

Shortly after *J'accuse* was published in Clemenceau's *L'Aurore,* the same paper carried 2 petitions, or open letters, against the original verdict against Dreyfus, and these were signed largely by academics, students and artists. The term "intellectuals" was mentioned by the paper, but it may have owed its widespread adoption to the fact that it was pejoratively used by anti-Dreyfusard writer Maurice Barrès.[1] Much of the development of the rest of the controversy in France took shape around what was seen as a conflict between the intellectuals on one side and the popular masses on the other[2], a dichotomy was employed by the right and which has often been so employed since then.[3]

It was not only writers who were deeply divided over the affair. Painters, as well as other artistic professions, were affected, with Monet and Pissarro coming out on the Dreyfusard side, while Cézanne, Degas and Renoir were anti-Dreyfusard.[4] Indeed, a list of prominent anti-Dreyfusards in France at the time would be quite likely to throw up as big a contingent of "intellectuals" as the Dreyfusard.

Abroad, intellectuals or "intelligentsia" were not yet popularly perceived as such, but it is nevertheless quite valid to study them collectively in historical hindsight. It would be fair to say that almost everywhere outside France, intellectuals considered the cause of Dreyfus, to use a modern term, a "no-brainer."

However, it must also be said that pronouncements on the *affaire* from Ireland's intellectuals were not numerous, though some information can be gleaned from various sources, especially biographies and correspondence. Those sources do not fall within the scope of this study, but it is worth mentioning a few which are available.

Yeats certainly counted himself a Dreyfusard, but perhaps one influenced by instincts similar to those which triggered his Parnellism. "Yeats was a Dreyfusard, Gonne Anti-Dreyfus" says one recent author. [5] The context here was of course hugely added to by Maud Gonne's residency in Paris, where she had cohabited with Lucien Millevoye, a leading nationalist and anti-Dreyfusard agitator. However, according to McCormack, it was the very unpopularity of the Dreyfusard cause which "...commended the Captain to Yeats, who had no inherited anti-Semitism to inhibit his allegiance." [6] Catholic, anti-Dreyfusard France was perhaps for Yeats and others a mirror-image of Catholic, anti-Parnellite Ireland.

Lady Gregory, on the other hand, seems to have had no instinctive sympathy with the Dreyfusard cause. While in Italy in late 1898, an acquaintance declared a hope that Dreyfus was innocent, to which Gregory replied "I say, in hoping that, you hope that a great many are guilty."[7] George Moore has been described by one biographer as a "mild Dreyfusard."[8]

The member of Ireland's intelligentsia one would think most likely to have expressed views on the affaire is the young James Joyce, a committed modernist whose work, in particular *Ulysses*, contains a clear expression of awareness of the presence of Jews in his own city. As Neil Davison says, "... Joyce lived through the Dreyfus affair, and knew many Jews who suffered the effects of political anti-Semitic platforms." [9] The affaire is briefly referred to in *Finnegans wake*.[10] However, although there is little doubt that Joyce read and knew much about the progress of the affaire in its later stages, and although it is likely that, as Davison says, this served to enhance Joyce's ill feelings towards the Church,[11] Joyce did not express any opinions on the issue, at least in writing.

Perhaps the most surprising Irish associate of the anti-Dreyfusard camp was Oscar Wilde, who had suffered a cruel imprisonment contemporaneously with Dreyfus and who was living in Paris at the height of the *affaire*. It seems likely that during his own imprisonment, Wilde had felt snubbed by Émile Zola, who, he believed, "...had refused to sign a petition circulated among men of letters in Paris for mitigation of his harsh criminal sentence." [12]

Wilde befriended and consorted with Esterhazy and an anti-Semitic group around him, but it does not follow that Wilde was an anti-Dreyfusard true believer. It is more likely that he developed these associations in spite of his associates' shortcomings. It has been said that "Wilde became fascinated by the wickedness and panache of Esterhazy – so much more attractive than the drabness and innocence of Dreyfus."[13] There were rumours (never proven) that Wilde had helped to warn Esterhazy about an imminent denunciation and release of incriminating documents by a Dreyfusard acquaintance, which would have helped incriminate him, and that this warning helped to stymie the move.[14]

J. M. Synge is another author who is not known to have commented on the *affaire* per se, but he did dream of Dreyfus and the *affaire* while he was in the Aran Islands at the time of the Rennes verdict. He was probably very knowledgeable about the issues involved, as he had been yet another member of the Irish expatriate community in 1898-9, about which one Synge biographer has commented "...it is fair to conclude that the Irish émigré circle in which Synge found himself occasionally embroiled during his Paris sojourns aligned to the radical right wing of French attitudes." [15]

There were few other prominent Irishmen who played any part in the *affaire* or its aftermath. One Irish influence within Britain was Lord Russell of Killowen, the Irish Catholic Lord Chief Justice and a confidant of Queen Victoria. Russell, who attended the Rennes Court-Martial and wrote a report for the Queen, was somewhat more restrained than most of the British establishment, and "criticised the rather too exaggerated reactions of the British press."[16]

Irish writers seem to have been relatively little influenced by the more radical political viewpoints then being developed on the Continent. Not only were there no Marxists of note, but even Irish radical nationalism had no strong echoes of the anti-liberal nationalism represented in France by Maurice Barrès or Charles Maurras. The closest disciples of such views were Frank Hugh O'Donnell and, arguably, D. P. Moran, whose *Leader* did not begin publication until 1900.

There are a number of other prominent Irish intellectuals whose views on the affaire are unknown, but it seems likely that Ireland's intelligentsia were, on the whole, not very different in their balance of opinions from their counterparts elsewhere in the Anglophone world.

Endnotes

1 See editors' introduction (p.6) of Datta V. and Silverman, W. (eds) *Intellectuals and the Dreyfus affair* (special issue, Historical reflections,/Reflexions historiques, vol.42 no.1, Spring 1998

2 See Forth, Eric *Intellectuals, crowds and the body politics of the Dreyfus Affair* in Datta and Silverman op.cit. pp.63-91.

3 "... the word, initially used derisively, applied to those who had cut themelves off from the organic body of France, who were losing their instints as French people by exercising their reason in defiance of national interests." Winock, M. *Nationalism, anti-Semitism and Fascism in France* (Stanford: Stanford University press, 1998)

4 See Nord, Philip *The new painting and the Dreyfus affair* in Datta and Silverman op. cit. pp.115-136.

5 McCormack, W.J. *Blood Kindred: W.B. Yeats the life, the death, the politics* London:Pimlico, 2005, p.343.

6 McCormack, W.J. Op cit. p.343.

7 Lady Gregory, 27 October 1898. *Diaries,* ed. J. Pethica (Colin Smythe, 1996), 27 October 1898, p.193.

8 Frazier, Adrian *George Moore, 1852-1933* (London: Yale University Press, 2000) p.265

9 Davison, Neil R. James Joyce, *Ulysses and the construction of the Jewish identity: culture, biography and "The Jew" in modernist Europe* (Cambridge: C.U.P. 1996) p.14.

10 For example the pun-word "Dreyschluss". See Nadel, I. *Joyce and the Jews: culture and texts* (Basingstoke: Macmillan, 1989) p.67.

11 See Davison, op. cit. p.72

12 Maguire, J. Robert Oscar Wilde and the Dreyfus affair in *Victorian Studies* 41(1) Fall 1997, p.20.

13 Hitchens, M. *Oscar Wilde's last chance: the Dreyfus connection* (Edinburgh: Pentland, 1999) p.146.

14 See Hitchens, op. cit.

15 McCormack, W. J. *Fool of the family: a life of J.M. Synge* London: Weidenfeld and Nicolson, 2000.

16 See Cornick, M. The impact of the Dreyfus affair in late-Victorian Britain in *Franco-British Studies* 22, Autumn 1996, p. 69-70.

"The honour of the army is saved":
Dreyfusard cartoon from the Irish Weekly Independent,
16 September 1899
(With permission of Independent Newspapers)

CONCLUSIONS

A writer on British opinions of the *affaire* has remarked that "The response of the British press to the Dreyfus Affaire tells us as much or more about the British as the French. One can almost say that the British looked at France and saw Britain."[1] Another writer on the same subject has remarked that "In England, the reaction to the Rennes trial had always been more anti-French than pro-Dreyfus."[2] The first writer's point is that the British tended to read their expectations of right and wrong into the affairs of their neighbours, and the second meant that England in 1898-99 was in an adversarial relationship with France. In passing, it may also be observed that it was England, not France, that was to pass legislation restricting Jewish immigration in 1905.

In counterpoint to this, one can say without difficulty that "The nationalist Irish looked at France and saw not-Britain." One can also say, but not say unreservedly, that "In nationalist Ireland, the reaction to the Rennes trial had always been more anti-British than anti-Dreyfus."

Certainly, the unsupportive tone shown by most of the nationalist press towards the Dreyfusard cause was almost certainly motivated mainly by feelings of wanting to get at the British, partly for their supposed hypocrisy in backing justice for Dreyfus while denying it to Irish political prisoners, and partly because of opposition to British policy in general which also animated the pro-Boer sentiment in Ireland at the time. The antagonism which existed at that point between Britain and France must certainly have engendered a feeling that "England's enemy is Ireland's friend," a variant of the nationalist mantra that "England's difficulty is Ireland's opportunity."

That does not necessarily mean that Irish nationalist views of the *affaire* would have been exactly the same if these events had happened in, say, Germany. British attacks on a nation perceived as Catholic were always more likely to bristle with nationalists whose sense of history owed a lot to the past oppression of Catholics, and at a time coinciding with the continuing attempt of Catholics to win concessions such as a Catholic university.

France was of course a much more complicated entity than simply a "Catholic nation." France was indeed the "eldest daughter of the Church," but she had also been the epicentre of the Enlightenment and a powerhouse of secularism and revolutionary politics. Relationships between the French Church and the Third Republic were still problematic at that time. Irish nationalist responses to events in France, however, did not neatly follow such a fault-line, because the Irish nationalist view of France implicitly reconciled, or perhaps glossed over, the opposing ideas of Catholic France as an old ally of the Irish Catholic cause, and revolutionary France as a provider of troops in 1798. We can see this reconciled view, for instance, in the fact that the Irish clergy seem to have had no difficulty with celebrations of French involvement in the 1798 rising when its centenary was celebrated in 1898.

An interesting trend was visible in a section of the nationalist press, especially outside Dublin. This was a sort of Catholic Dreyfusardism, apparently not inspired by liberalism or modernism, but by a religious critique of the secularised nature of French politics and society. According to this point of view, espoused by the *Kilkenny Journal* and others, the injustice done to Dreyfus showed that "Godless" France, by its worship of the Army and State, had lost its way.

That view apart, the question remains of whether the anti- or non- Dreyfusardism of much of the nationalist press was solely motivated by anti-British feeling or whether some of it would have existed anyway. The most plausible answer is that in some quarters it probably would have. The Catholic press, for example was undoubtedly influenced by the opinions of its French as much as if not more than its English counterparts, and in any case many Irish nationalists, asked to choose between the Catholic, authoritarian France of Joan of Arc and the liberal republican France of *Marianne,* would probably have felt more comfortable with the former.

France fared less well in the eyes of the unionist press. France and her people were referred to in unionist editorials as having a depressed moral tone; she was going to find herself lowered in the estimation of other nations, she must be taken to task before the whole world, and her people's national amusements included almost daily perjury and forgery. Comments of this kind may have been motivated by moral indignation, but even so, it also seems likely that they were made with greater relish at the time of Fashoda.

Of course most (but not all) of the unionist press shared the Dreyfusism of their British counterparts. For those that did, it is not at all obvious that the stance of the unionist press was motivated solely by considerations of British foreign policy or by a complacent sense of Anglo-Saxon superiority, and the tone in particular of the *Irish Times* letters page contributions reflects a genuinely felt sense of outrage on the part of the writers. However, it is not possible to discount an anti-Catholic or anti-nationalist motivation for some of the point-scoring by the Northern unionist press

Nevertheless, support for a boycott of the 1900 exhibition, even among the most pro-Dreyfus papers, was low and patchy. The unionist *Irish Times* for example opposed it, and the nationalist *Limerick Leader* was one of the only papers to support it.

The next obvious question to consider is that of anti-Semitism.

When considering the incidence of anti-Semitism in the anti-Dreyfusard newspapers in Ireland, a distinction could be argued between two levels or types of anti-Semitism.

At the more anti-Semitic extreme, a racialist anti-Semitic line was taken by *United Ireland* and by Griffith's *United Irishman*. In both of these papers, most of the virulently anti-Semitic articles seem to have been penned by Frank Hugh O'Donnell, probably the only Irish writer of the period whose views are comparable to those of continental extremists such as Édouard Drumont. The same views are also apparent in the *Irish News* in 1898 (though not the following year at the time of Rennes) and in Jasper Tully's *Roscommon Herald*. In these there were out-and-out denunciations of Jews as parasitic, anti-national and deserving of exclusion from public life.

Of slightly lesser degree would be the anti-Semitism of the main nationalist dailies, such as the *Irish Daily Independent, Freeman's Journal* and *Daily Nation*, plus the *Irish Catholic*. These papers portrayed French Jews as an organised interest group, with the clear implication that the "syndicate" spoken of by French anti-Dreyfusards was a reality. For the Catholic papers, the Jews were willing participants in an unholy coalition with Freemasons and Atheists aimed at root and branch secularisation of the oldest daughter of the Church. These papers, however, tended to "balance" such statements by denouncing the blood libel, and also by dichotomising between "honest" defenders of Dreyfus and more extreme forces whose main aim was to damage the Church.

The allegedly vast power of the Jews was not ascribed only to France. Part of the reason for the pro-Dreyfus slant taken by the English press, according to the *Daily Nation* and others, was that they, as well as the wire services, were Jewish-controlled. The *Daily Nation* was in no doubt that the Jews as a group carefully balanced their support for the Dreyfusard cause, with the attendant risk of national destabilisation and even of revolution, against their hard-nosed collective business interests. The *Irish Daily Independent* stated that the French people perceived the Jews as having too much power and wealth, and that the French people's perceptions on matters of this kind were seldom wrong.

This group of papers was clearly expressing anti-Semitic prejudice, but it might be argued that this anti-Semitism was employed opportunistically, rather than out of deep conviction, as a means of defending France, or a version of France, from allegedly hypocritical and selective attacks by their British opposite numbers.

The anti-Dreyfusardism of Griffith, Maud Gonne, Arthur Lynch and others is not easy to characterise. It is not easily accounted for by Catholic conservatism, as this group included anti-clericals and unrepentant Parnellites. It may be supposed, even in the absence of documentary evidence, that in those instances, influences of racial nationalism from mainland Europe were at work. Apart from that, the Parnellite press tended to be more Dreyfusard and less anti-Semitic than the more clericalist anti-Parnellite press.

Mention must also be made of the line taken by Michael Davitt, who, as we have seen, believed that the campaign on Dreyfus's behalf was mounted at the behest of powerful Jewish interests, and that this happened mainly because Dreyfus was a Jew. Davitt undoubtedly subscribed, in 1899 at any rate, to assumptions about Jews which were prevalent in "advanced" nationalist circles.

Attitudes which would strike people nowadays as questionable, or even bizarre, were expressed on the pro-Jewish and pro-Dreyfusard side as well. The correspondent "I.V.Y."

in *United Ireland*, who was writing to object to O'Donnell's anti-Semitism, said he himself would never vote for a Jew, and thought that the establishment of the Ghetto in Rome was a justifiable measure intended to protect Jews. Some strong support for Dreyfus and the Jews was advanced by the Protestant Irish Mission to the Jews, both in 1899 and later during the Limerick Jewish Boycott. However, the reasons for this were not simple philosemitism. This body hoped to convert the Jews, and claimed that Jews instinctively respected and preferred reformed Protestant Christianity to Catholicism.

If we try to relate the anti-Semitism shown by Irish newspapers on the *affaire* to the situation in Ireland, it must be observed that there is no known case of the Dreyfus affair being used in connection with any anti-Semitic incident within Ireland, or of events at the time in France being used at any time to justify hostility to Irish Jews.

There are only a few very minor cases where differing unionist and nationalist views on the case were a cause of friction between the two camps, which contrasts with the stronger and more vehement divisions that were engendered by the Boer crisis of the same year.

Do the opinions we have seen on the *affaire* offer any clues as to whether the Irish at this time were more, or less, anti-Semitic than other peoples? Certainly, a look at the range of nationalist opinions would suggest that a significant amount of prejudice against Jews existed, and the perception that Jews on the continent were a powerful and privileged community whose members helped each other, and who were enemies of the Catholic Church, was widely shared.

A look at unionist opinions would conversely suggest that Ireland's Protestants were free of anti-Semitic feeling. However, it has to be remembered that Britain's apparent philosemitism at this time was almost as opportunistic as the anti-Dreyfusism of the nationalists, and it is likely that anti-Jewish prejudice was usually stronger in Britain. It would therefore still be reasonable to say that Ireland was not a strongly anti-Semitic country.

Also worth remarking on is the absence of any sign of a collective intelligentsia response in Ireland to the *affaire*. Dreyfusardism among Ireland's intelligentsia could not be taken for granted to the extent that it could be in Britain, but only in a very few cases do we have any expressions of opinion by Irish intellectuals, either established ones or up and coming ones.

If one is looking for a relatively close parallel with the way the *affaire* was discussed in Britain as against Ireland, the answer could be Canada. Canada was a predominantly Anglo-Saxon and Protestant jurisdiction which happened to contain a geographically and ethno-religiously discrete minority, namely francophone Québec, where Catholicism and nationalistic aspirations were also blended. Unsurprisingly, opinions in Canada on the *affaire* differed in a way that is analogous to those between Britain and Ireland, or between Protestant Ulster and Catholic Ireland. The "British" point of view, and similar features of interest within that point of view, can be seen in the press of Anglophone Western Canada, where press opinion echoed British and Ulster protestant assumptions of Anglo-Saxon superiority, for example, the Calgary *Herald* describing the French nation as "rotten both politically and socially."[3]

In Québec , differences over the *affaire* mirrored those in Ireland, with Anglophones as Dreyfusards and Francophones going the other way. Québec 's Anglophone papers "...seized the opportunity to emphasize the differences between France and England, the two "mother countries" of Canada, and thus also between French Canada and British Canada."[4] In contrast, the Francophone *La Presse,* like the *Irish Daily Independent,* defended the Dreyfus trials as fair.[5] Québécois nationalists, like many Irish nationalists, saw the Catholic faith, along with their language, as being an essential part of their identity.[6]

In any case, it is a fact that taken as a whole, the Irish press was the most anti-Dreyfusard of any in the English-speaking world, and Dublin can safely be regarded as the only real stronghold in the English-speaking world of anti-Dreyfusism. Among Catholic nations Ireland was not untypical in the pattern of opinions on the affair, even though Ireland was untypical among Catholic countries in not having the same politico-cultural split between secular-liberals and clerical-conservatives that characterised other Catholic countries at the time.

The discussion of the Dreyfus affair in the Irish nationalist press contained significant elements of anti-Semitism, but this was far from universal and was frequently opposed. Much more pervasive was a willingness by the nationalist press to cavil at, and turn their backs on, the campaign for justice for Dreyfus, a campaign almost universally endorsed elsewhere, in order to advance their own political agenda.

Endnotes

1   Sherrod, Ricky Lee *Images and reflections: the response of the British press to the Dreyfus Affaire* (PhD, Michigan State University, 1980), p.253

2   Huch, Ronald British reaction to the Dreyfus affair in *Social Science*, Winter 1975 p.23 (quoted in Sherrod, op cit p.260.

3   See Senese, Phullis M. Antisemitic Dreyfusards: the confused Western-Canadian press IN Davies, A. (ed.) *Antisemitism in Canada: history and interpretation* (Waterloo, Ont.: Wilfrid Laurier University press, 1992) p. 93-111 (above q. from p.100)

4   See Brown, M. From stereotype to scapegoat: Anti-Jewish sentiment in French Canada from Confederation to World War 1 in Davies, A. op cit p.39-66 (above q. p. 48.)

5   See Brown, M. op cit p.49. This author also points out Québec also had its local versions of *La Croix* and *La Libre Parole*, and the father of Québec separatism, Henri Bourassa, had anti-Semitic tendencies.

6   See Brown op cit. p.59.

BIBLIOGRAPHY

Primary sources

Newspapers

Irish nationalist newspapers

An Claidheamh Soluis
Cork Examiner
Daily Nation
Evening Herald
Freeman's Journal (Dublin)
Irish Daily Independent
Irish News (Belfast)
Irish Weekly Independent
Kerry Sentinel
Kilkenny Journal
Limerick Leader
Nationalist and Leinster Times (Carlow)
Roscommon Herald
Roscommon Journal
Sligo Champion
United Ireland
United Irishman
Waterford News
Weekly Nation
Workers' Republic

Irish unionist newspapers

Belfast Newsletter
Carlow Sentinel
Cork Constitution
Daily Express (Dublin)
Derry Standard
Eagle and County Cork advertiser
(Skibbereen)
Evening Mail
Evening Telegraph (Belfast)
Irish Society
Irish Times
Londonderry Sentinel
Meath Herald
Northern Whig

Irish religious periodicals

Irish Catholic
Irish Ecclesiastical record
Irish Rosary
Lyceum
New Ireland review

Expatriate periodicals

Freeman's Journal (Sydney)
Irish American (New York)
Irish World (New York)
Pilot (Boston)
Southern Cross (Buenos Aires)

Other primary sources

Lady Gregory, *Diaries,* ed. J. Pethica (Colin Smythe, 1996)

Logue, Michael (Cardinal) – Logue papers, Armagh diocesan archives

Walsh, William J. – Archbishop Walsh papers in Dublin diocesan archives

Secondary sources

The Dreyfus affair in general and its significance

Datta V. and Silverman, W. (eds), Intellectuals and the Dreyfus affair (special issue, *Historical reflections,/Reflexions historiques*, vol.42 no.1, Spring 1998).

Begley, Louis, Why the Dreyfus affair matters (Yale University Press, 2010)

Forth, C. E., The Dreyfus affair and the crisis of French manhood (Baltimore, MD: Johns Hopkins University Press, 2004)
Forth, C. E. Intellectuals, crowds and the body politics of the Dreyfus affair *in* Datta and Silverman, op. cit. p.63-91

Harris, Ruth, The man on Devil's Island: Alfred Dreyfus and the affair that divided France (London: Allen Lane, 2010)

Guieu, J-M., Chronology of the Dreyfus affair [online] at http://www9.georgetown.edu/faculty/guieuj/DreyfusCase/Chronology%20of%20the%20Dreyfus%20Affair.htm Viewed 21 April 2010

Johnson, M. P., The Dreyfus affair: honour and politics in the Belle époque (Palgrave Macmillan, 1999)

Larkin, Maurice, Church and state after the Dreyfus affair: the separation issue in France (Macmillan 1974)

Nord, P. The new painting and the Dreyfus affair *in* Datta and Silverman, op. cit. p.115-136.

Public opinion on the *affaire*

Brennan, J. F., The reflection of the Dreyfus affair in the European press, 1897-1899 (New York: Peter Lang, 1998)

Brown, M., From stereotype to scapegoat: Anti-Jewish sentiment in French Canada from Confederation to World War 1 *in* Davies,

A. (ed.) Antisemitism in Canada: history and interpretation (Waterloo, Ont.: Wilfrid Laurier University Press, 1992) p.39-66

Cornick, M., The impact of the Dreyfus affair in late-Victorian Britain *Franco-British studies* 22, Autumn 1996, p. 69-70.

Denis, M., Lagree, M., Veillard, J-Y (eds), L'affaire Dreyfus et l'opinion publique en France et a l'étranger (Rennes: Presses Universitaires de Rennes, 1995)

Feldman, Egal, The Dreyfus affair and the American conscience, 1895-1906 (Detroit: Wayne State University Press, 1981

Senese, Phyllis M. Antisemitic Dreyfusards: the confused Western-Canadian press *in* Davies, A. Op. cit. p.93-111

Sherrod, Ricky Lee, Images and reflections: the response of the British press to the Dreyfus Affaire (PhD, Michigan State University, 1980)

Thornton-Smith, C. Reactions of the Australian Catholic press to the Dreyfus case in *Australian Jewish Historical Society Journal*, 1997(14), 57 at 64

Tombs, Robert, "Lesser Breeds without the law": the British establishment and the Dreyfus affair 1894-99 *Historical Journal* 41(2) p.495-510

Ireland at the time of the *affaire*

Garvin, Tom, The evolution of Irish nationalist politics (Dublin: Gill and Macmillan, 1981)

Lyons, F.S.L. Ireland since the famine (London: Weidenfeld and Nicolson, 1971)

Maume, Patrick, The long gestation: Irish nationalist life 1891-1918 (Dublin: Gill and Macmillan, 1999)

The Irish newspaper industry

Legg, Marie-Louise, Newspapers and nationalism: the Irish provincial press, 1852-1892 (Dublin: Four Courts, 1999)

Morash, Christopher, A history of the media in Ireland (Cambridge: C.U.P., 2010)

Irish individuals involved in or influenced by the *affaire*

Cardozo, Nancy, Maud Gonne: lucky eyes and a high heart (London: Victor Gollancz, 1979)

Davison, Neil R., James Joyce, Ulysses and the construction of the Jewish identity: culture, biography and "The Jew" in modernist Europe (Cambridge: C.U.P. 1996)

Hitchens, M., Oscar Wilde's last chance: the Dreyfus connection (Edinburgh: Pentland, 1999)

McCormack, W.J., Blood kindred: W.B. Yeats the life, the death, the politics (London: Pimlico, 2005)

McCormack, W. J., Fool of the family: a life of J.M. Synge (London: Weidenfeld and Nicolson, 2000?)

Maguire, J. Robert, Oscar Wilde and the Dreyfus affair in *Victorian studies* 41(1) Fall 1997

Marley, Laurence, Michael Davitt: freelance radical and frondeur (Dublin: Four Courts Press, 2007)

Martin, F. X. The writings of Eoin Mac Neill in *Irish Historical Studies,* vol.6 no.21, March 1948, p.44-62

Maye, Brian, Arthur Griffith (Dublin: Griffith College Publications, 1997)

Nadel, I., Joyce and the Jews: culture and texts (Basingstoke: Macmillan, 1989)

Nevin, Donal, James Connolly: "a full life" (Dublin: Gill and Macmillan, 2005)

O'Brien, R. Barry, The life of Lord Russell of Killowen (London: Smith, Elder: 1901

Tierney, Michael, Eoin Mac Neill: scholar and man of action, 1867-1945 (Oxford: Clarendon Press, 1980)

Walsh, Patrick J. William J. Walsh: Archbishop of Dublin (Cork: Talbot Press, 1927)

Jews, Jewish affairs and anti-Semitism

Keogh, Dermot and McCarthy, Andrew, Limerick boycott: anti-Semitism in Ireland (Cork: Mercier Press, 2005)

Keogh, Dermot, Jews in twentieth-century Ireland: refugees, anti-Semitism and the holocaust (Cork University Press, 1998)

O Grada, Cormac, Jewish Ireland in the age of Joyce: a socioeconomic history (Princeton University Press, 2006)

Shillman, Bernard, A short history of the Jews in Ireland (Dublin: Cahill-Eason, 1945)

Wilson, S., Ideology and experience: anti-Semitism in France at the time of the Dreyfus affair (London: Associated University presses, 1982)

Winock, M., Nationalism, anti-Semitism and Fascism in France (Stanford: Stanford University Press, 1998)

INDEX

Journal titles are in *italics*. Pseudonyms are in quotes